Mixed Categories in the Hierarchical Lexicon

Studies in Constraint-Based Lexicalism

A series edited by
Miriam Butt, *University of Konstanz*
Andreas Kathol, *University of California, Berkeley*
Tracy Holloway King, *Xerox Palo Alto Research Center*
Jean-Pierre Koenig, *State University of New York at Buffalo*
Sam Mchombo, *University of California, Berkeley*

The aim of this series is to make work in various nonderivational, lexicalist approaches to grammar available to a wide audience of linguists. In approaches of this kind, grammar is seen as the interaction of constraints from multiple dimensions of linguistic substance, including information about syntactic category, grammatical relations, and semantic and pragmatic interpretation.

Studies in
Constraint-Based Lexicalism

Mixed Categories in the Hierarchical Lexicon

Robert P. Malouf

CSLI Publications
CENTER FOR THE STUDY OF
LANGUAGE AND INFORMATION
STANFORD, CALIFORNIA

Library of Congress Cataloging-in-Publication Data

Malouf, Robert P., 1969-
    Mixed categories in the hierarchical lexicon/ Robert P. Malouf.
    p. cm. -- (Studies in constraint-based lexicalism)
    Originally presented as the author's thesis.
    Includes bibliographical references and indexes.
    ISBN 1-57586-191-7 (alk. paper) -- ISBN 1-57586-190-9 (pbk. : alk.
paper)
    1. Grammar, Comparative and general--Grammatical categories. 2.
Grammar, Comparative and general--Syntax. 3. Lexicology. 4. Hierarchy
(Linguistics) 5. Generative grammar. I. Title. II. Series.
    P240.5.M35 1999
    415--dc21
                                            99-13308
                                            CIP

∞ The acid-free paper used in this book meets the minimum requirements of the
American National Standard for Information Sciences – Permanence of Paper for
Printed Library Materials, ansi z39.48-1984.

Please visit our web site at
http://cslipublications.stanford.edu/
for comments on this and other titles, as well as for changes
and corrections by the authors, editors and publisher.

Contents

Acknowledgments

This book is a revised version of my 1998 Stanford University Ph.D. thesis. I am deeply indebted to my committee, Ivan Sag, Peter Sells, Elizabeth Traugott, and Tom Wasow. In addition, Farrell Ackerman and Gert Webelhuth provided invaluable comments and criticisms throughout the development of this work. I have also benefited from many fruitful discussions with Arto Anttila, Jennifer Arnold, Ann Copestake, Emily Bender, Bob Borsley, Matthew Dryer, Dan Flickinger, Vivienne Fong, Jong-Bok Kim, Chris Manning, Yukiko Morimoto, Susanne Riehemann, Richard Schupbach, Martine Smets, Julie Solomon, Ida Toivonen, Michael Wescoat, Arnold Zwicky, and my colleagues at the Center for the Study of Language and Information, UC Berkeley, and the University of Groningen. For help in revising my thesis into the present form, I am grateful to Kim Lewis Brown, Maureen Burke, Tony Gee, Dikran Karagueuzian, and Tom Wasow for their wisdom and patience.

While at Stanford, I was supported by graduate fellowships from the National Science Foundation and the Stanford University linguistics department. Further development of these ideas was conducted in part under the auspices of CSLI's Linguistic Grammars On-line (LinGO) project, made possible by the Bundesministerium für Bildung, Wissenschaft, Forschung, und Technologie (Project VERBMOBIL) and the National Science Foundation (grant number IRI-9612682). The final preparation of this volume was supported by the School of Behavioral and Cognitive Neurosciences at the University of Groningen.

Last and foremost, I'd like to thank Deirdre and James for standing by me and for keeping me sane.

1

Introduction

1.1 Overview

English nominalizations like the verbal gerunds in (1) have played an important role in the development of generative grammar since its earliest days (Lees 1960).

(1) a. Pat's washing the car
    b. Pat washing the car

These constructions simultaneously show some of the properties of noun phrases and some of the properties of verb phrases. This has generally been taken as evidence that these constructions are verb phrases at one level and noun phrases at another.

In this book I will defend an alternative view. I will show that the hybrid properties of constructions like (1) follow from the lexical properties of their heads, just as in any other endocentric phrase. What makes verbal gerunds different from 'normal' NPs and VPs is that they are headed by words that belong to a **mixed category** and have some of the lexical properties of more than one part of speech.

In the remainder of this chapter, I will sketch the general theoretical background against which this is an interesting problem and outline Head-driven Phrase Structure Grammar (HPSG), the specific theoretical framework I will be assuming in my analysis. In the second chapter, I will describe the properties of English verbal gerunds in more detail, summarize previous accounts of them in the literature, and propose a first attempt at an analysis of (1) as a mixed category construction. Constructions like the verbal gerund are quite common in the world's languages, so in the third chapter I will review the range of cross-linguistic variation and revise my analysis to account for it. Finally, in the fourth chapter I will offer some conclusions as to the theoretical consequences of this approach for HPSG and for linguistics in general.

1.2   Background

Grammatical categories are central to generative theories of grammar. In many ways, the study of syntax really is just the study of grammatical categories. However, despite their importance, relatively little attention has been paid to investigating the essential nature of grammatical categories. It is typically assumed that there is a small number of primitive, probably universal, probably innate grammatical categories. This assumption is made quite explicitly by Chomsky (1965, 65f):

> The question of substantive representation in the case of the grammatical formatives and the category symbols is, in effect, the traditional question of universal grammar. I shall assume that these elements too are selected from a fixed, universal vocabulary, although this assumption will actually have no significant effect on any of the descriptive material to be presented.

Attention has turned in more recent work to decomposing primitive category labels into a small universal set of binary features (Chomsky 1970) but the fundamental enterprise has not changed. A second assumption about grammatical categories that is common among generative grammarians is that the properties of a phrase are primarily determined by the category of its head. That is, a verb phrase has the properties of a verb phrase by virtue of its being headed by a verb. The origins of this second assumption are less obvious. It is never explicitly stated and does not seem to follow necessarily from anything else about generative theories of grammar. Indeed, as the field has moved from *Aspects*-style transformational grammar to more modular theories over the last twenty years, it has become possible to attribute the properties of a phrase to, say, the Case-assigning potential and the theta grid of its lexical head. However, grammatical sub-theories are defined in terms of the primitive syntactic categories (e.g., Case is assigned under government by a [−N] head), and the analytic possibilities opened up by richer lexical representations are rarely exploited.

This view of parts of speech is in large part a legacy of traditional grammar, apparently adopted at least at first as a working hypothesis in need of further refinement. Chomsky (1975) discusses some of the shortcomings of the purely distributional approach to categories favored by American structuralists, but offers no substantive theory of categories of his own. Instead, he takes a set of basic categories as given: "The primes of **P** will be labeled so as to suggest their customary names (e.g., *NP, V,* etc.)" (223).

The problems with naively applying the traditional part of speech distinctions to typologically diverse languages were well known. Whorf (1945, 1) warned that "the very natural tendency to use terms derived from traditional grammar, like verb, noun, adjective, passive voice, in describing languages outside of Indo-European is fraught with grave possibilities of misunderstanding". Chomsky (1965) acknowledges the potential dangers of positing a universal set of categories from those of English. However, he points out in a footnote that the "study of a wide range of languages is only one of the ways to evaluate the hypothesis that some formal condition is a linguistic universal" (209) and expresses the hope that the study of English at a highly abstract level would be sufficient to justify a set of universal categories.

Since the advent of generative grammar, linguists have made considerable progress in the understanding of language. Not surprisingly, the traditional inventory of parts of speech has proven to be sufficient for the analysis of most constructions in English and for a broad range of other languages. Certain problems that have cropped up with the parts of speech that were originally proposed have been solved by decomposing them into bundles of binary features, allowing categories to be divided into subcategories and to be grouped into natural classes (Chomsky 1970).

However, there is a class of constructions, known as **transcategorial** or simply mixed category constructions, which do not fit well with any refinement of the four basic categories. These constructions involve lexical items which seem to be core members of more than one category simultaneously. A well-known example is the English verbal gerund, which combines with both a direct object (like a verb does) and a genitive possessor (like a noun does).

Several alternatives to the traditional system of parts of speech have been proposed. Sapir (1921, 118f) clearly rejects the notion of parts of speech as syntactic primitives:

> A part of speech outside of the limitations of syntactic form is but a will o' the wisp. For this reason, no logical scheme of the parts of speech—their number, nature, and necessary confines—is of the slightest interest to the linguist.

More moderately, Bloomfield (1933, 196) warns against what he saw as the practice of traditional grammarians:

> The term *parts of speech* is traditionally applied to the most inclusive and fundamental word-classes of a language, and then [...] the syntactic form classes are described in terms of the parts of speech that appear in them. However, it is

impossible to set up a fully consistent set of parts of speech, because the word-classes overlap and cross each other.

Bloomfield is not arguing against a set of either universal or language-particular parts of speech, but against the very idea of parts of speech as anything but vague generalizations across overlapping word classes.

For the most part, the structuralists' concerns have been ignored by generative grammarians. Chomsky's adoption of traditional parts of speech marks a clear break with earlier practice. One notable exception is McCawley (1982), who argues for an approach to parts of speech that "... avoids the notion of syntactic category as such, operating instead directly in terms of a number of distinct factors which syntactic phenomena can be sensitive to; in this view, syntactic category names will merely be informal abbreviations for combinations of these factors" (185). McCawley goes on to identify a number of dimensions of categoriality, including semantic type, grammatical function, exception features (such as AUX), and lexical category (i.e., N, V, A, ...). While McCawley's view of categories cannot be described as structuralist by any means, he shares with Bloomfield a generally 'bottom-up' direction of inquiry. Rather than taking a set of categories as given and setting out to discover their properties, McCawley proposes to concentrate instead on the properties themselves. Only after the range of syntactic properties are better understood can we begin to see which properties cluster together.

A similar approach to categories was taken independently by Pollard and Sag (1987). In the course of describing Head-driven Phrase Structure Grammar (HPSG), an elaborated theory of syntactic information in terms of feature structures, they observe: "equipped with the notions of head features and subcategorization, we are now in a position to *define* conventional grammatical symbols such as NP, VP, etc. in terms of feature structures of type sign" (68). They offer the following definition for 'VP':

(2) $$\begin{bmatrix} \text{SYN} \,|\, \text{LOC} \,|\, \text{HEAD} \,|\, \text{MAJ } verb \\ \text{SUBCAT } \langle \text{NP} \rangle \end{bmatrix}$$

The diagram in (2) is an example of an attribute-value matrix (AVM), a representation for complex bundles of features. In this case, the value of the feature SUBCAT is a list consisting of a single NP, and the value of the path SYN|LOC|HEAD|MAJ (i.e., the value of the feature MAJ of the value of the feature HEAD of the value of the feature LOC of the value of the feature SYN) is the atomic value *verb*.

This decomposition of a syntactic category into features is quite different from the kind found in most statements of X-bar theory. Rather than making a more fine-grained distinction between categories in a single dimension (say, by adding more head features), (2) defines 'VP' in terms of two independently varying dimensions of syntactic information. 'VP' is distinguished from 'V' directly in terms of selectional saturation rather than indirectly via the interaction of subcategorization, phrase structure rules, and a categorial notion of bar level. And, 'VP' is distinguished from 'NP' by its lexical category (represented by the feature HEAD).

Furthermore, generalizations about feature structures in HPSG can be expressed formally via a type hierarchy. So, if it turns out that the grammar of English needs to make frequent reference to the feature values in (2), then they can be reified as types, as in (3).

(3) a. *verbal* →

$\left[\text{SYN} \mid \text{LOC} \mid \text{HEAD} \mid \text{MAJ } verb \right]$

b. *subject-seeking* →

$\left[\text{SUBCAT } \langle \text{NP} \rangle \right]$

These constraints can be read as implications: if the type of an object is *verbal* or a subtype of *verbal*, then the value of the path SYN|LOC|-HEAD|MAJ must be *verb*. A type representing the combination of feature values in (2) then can be defined as a subtype of the types *verbal* and *subject-seeking* which inherits both of the constraints in (3).

The use of types in HPSG solves a potential problem with McCawley's proposal, namely that it is not always possible to describe grammatical processes directly in terms of observable properties (cf. Whorf's (1945) cryptotypes). For example, take the class of transitive verbs in English. Both *remain* and *kiss* can occur without a direct object:

(4) a. Pat remained at the party too long.
    b. Pat kissed at the party too long.

But *kiss* can be passivized while *remain* cannot:

(5) a. *Pat was remained at the party.
    b. Pat was kissed at the party.

This shows that intransitivity of the verbs in (4) cannot be inferred simply from the absence of a direct object. Instead, transitive verbs must be distinguished from intransitive verbs by their valence, a more abstract property. In essence, HPSG's types correspond to Bloomfield's overlapping word classes.

In contrast to the strictly extensional, discrete view of categories common in generative grammar, functional and cognitive approaches to language have developed theories of prototype categories (e.g., Lakoff

1987, Langacker 1987a, Croft 1991, Taylor 1995). Quite unlike generative grammar's parts of speech (or HPSG's types), prototype categories allow gradient membership and have indistinct boundaries. Rather than sorting linguistic units into larger or smaller discrete, uniform classes, functionally oriented linguists instead explore the variation within heterogeneous classes.

Croft (1991) frames the difference between the two views of categories as a difference in the interpretation of morphosyntactic tests. A morphosyntactic test is a "grammatical construction, one or more features of which define or require a specific type of linguistic unit to satisfy it or fill it" (6). For example, in English only nouns can be pluralized through the addition of the suffix -s. Thus, the plural suffix can be used as a test for nounhood. We might take occurrence with the definite article the as another test for nounhood in English.

Ideally, all morphosyntactic tests for a particular linguistic unit in all languages will give the same result, but this is rarely the case. Croft argues that formal and functional approaches to linguistics diverge in their reconciliation of the ideal behavior of syntactic tests with their actual behavior. Generative grammarians take certain tests to be criterial, while dismissing other conflicting tests as peripheral or unreliable. This preserves the ideal view of categories as universal and discrete domains at the cost of "cut[ting] the link between the tests (i.e., features of grammatical constructions) and their domain of application (i.e., the class of linguistic units that those features admit)" (15).

For instance, the English word child can occur with the but cannot combine with plural -s. A formal linguist might take occurrence with the as criterial for nounhood, and classify child as a noun. Cognitive grammarians, on the other hand, "give up clear-cut distinctions between categories for prototypical organizations of categories" (16). Since child has one nounish property but not the other, a cognitive linguist might argue that child is a noun, but a less central example of a noun than, say, book.

Each of these compromises gives something up. In this study, I would like to argue for a third strategy for resolving this problem which preserves the best features of both formal and functional approaches. I will argue that the reason why different syntactic tests pick out different classes of linguistic units is simply that the tests pick out different grammatical categories. To return to our example, the class of linguistic units which can occur with the and the class of linguistic units that can occur with -s form two different grammatical categories (which happen to have substantial overlap). This allows categories to be treated as discrete and well-defined while still respecting the tight link between empirical observations and theoretical categories.

A consequence of this third approach is that grammatical categories must be much more numerous and much less general than is commonly assumed. In essence, this is a rejection of the validity of parts of speech as first-class linguistic categories. Instead, grammatical processes are sensitive to a number of independently varying types of information.

This is not to say that every lexical item must be listed in the lexicon *sui generis*. The lexicon is structured by a system of cross-cutting hierarchical types placing constraints on one or more of these dimensions of syntactic information. What remains to be explained then is why certain sets of word classes have significant overlap while others are disjoint, and why the same sets of overlapping word classes tend to be found in language after language. It may be true that in principle dimensions like lexical category, semantic type, and valence can vary independently, and I do believe that further investigation will reveal that mixed categorial behavior is more common than is typically appreciated. However, it remains a fact that in practice these dimensions almost always covary. 'Normal' nouns do not take accusative subjects or objects, and 'normal' verbs do not take genitive specifiers. Any grammatical theory that treats this as an accident of the English lexicon is probably missing something.

I will claim that parts of speech exist, but are external to the synchronic grammar. That is, a syntactic category like "noun", in the traditional sense, does not correspond to any one lexical type, but instead is more like a region within the hierarchical lexicon. This does not mean abandoning formal grammar: each individual type is still discrete and determinate (see Newmeyer 1998, 2000). It is only these second order generalizations over types that are vague. It also does not mean giving up on functionalist goals. Even though parts of speech are not first class objects in the synchronic grammar, there are universal affinities among certain word classes, and these collections of functionally related word classes can best be described as forming prototype categories. Formalist methods are best at describing in detail exactly what a language is like with enough precision that, for example, a grammar could be implemented as a computer program. Functionalist methods are best at explaining the patterns of variation within individual languages and across all languages. I hope what I will develop here will be able to take advantage of the best of both approaches.

1.3 HPSG preliminaries

An ideal analysis of mixed categories would be able to account for their hybrid properties without the addition of otherwise unmotivated mechanisms. Recent work in Construction Grammar (Zwicky 1994, Goldberg 1995, Fillmore and Kay to appear, Kay and Fillmore 1999) and Head-driven Phrase Structure Grammar (Pollard and Sag 1987, Pollard and Sag 1994) provides the foundation for such an analysis. In this section, I will present a brief overview of the relevant features of HPSG.

1.3.1 Goals of linguistic theory

Before going into the specifics of HPSG, it might be worthwhile to consider the larger question of what general goals HPSG is intended to achieve. First and foremost, HPSG is a constraint-based theory of grammar. As such, it shares a set of basic methodological goals and assumptions with a family of related frameworks

To see more clearly what specifically a constraint-based theory of grammar is, we can approach it compositionally. In this context, a grammar is the system of knowledge that speakers have when they "know" a language. In other words, the grammar is a person's linguistic competence, a system of knowledge independent of any particular use that knowledge might be put to.

Now, what about constraint-based? Consider how grammaticality judgements work: native speakers take a set of sentences and, using their grammatical knowledge, choose which ones are valid sentences of the language (i.e., which ones are grammatical) and which are not. A constraint-based approach to grammar works the same way. Given representations of linguistic objects, the grammar is a set of constraints that determine which linguistic objects correspond to grammatical sentences and which do not. This contrasts with derivational theories of grammar, which provide a set of instructions for constructing all and only representations for grammatical sentences.

Finally, what makes something a theory? This is a thorny question, as many different kinds of linguistic enterprises are described as "theories". Given that things as diverse as Optimality Theory and the reconstruction of Nostratic are called theories, it is unlikely that there can be any single characterization of what constitutes a linguistic theory. However, in the context of constraint-based theories of grammar, Pollard (1996) argues that an acceptable theory must meet eight basic criteria:

Generativity Above all, a theory of grammar should be generative, in Chomsky's (1957) original sense. This means three things. First, the notion "structural representation" must be effective. That is, there must be some way of determining whether or not some arbitrary set of symbols is or is not a possible structure in the theory. Second, the notion "constraint" must be effective. There must be some way of determining whether some arbitrary set of symbols is or is not a constraint, rule, or principle of the theory. Third, the notion "generates" must be effective. There must be some way of determining whether or not some structural representation is or is not admitted by a given set of constraints.

These are just the minimum requirements for something to be a theory, in the logical sense (see Pullum 1989). Anything that does not meet these criteria cannot really be called a theory (again, in this narrow sense), even though it may be informative and insightful. For example, autosegmental phonology provides no formal characterization of representations or constraints, and so does not meet this minimum standard. That is not to say that autosegmental phonology is not worth doing, only that it is not a constraint-based theory of grammar by these criteria.

Expressivity The metalanguage or formalism used to state a theory should be expressively rich and should not impose any unnecessary constraints on possible grammars. Suitable metalanguages include first order logic, the logic of typed feature structures, Prolog, English, etc. Note that this goes against the tendency in generative linguistics to require formalisms to be restrictive. The approach taken in constraint-based formalisms has been to depend on the particular theory of language to provide the constraints on possible grammars, not the metalanguage the theory is stated in.

Empirical adequacy This just means you need to get the facts right. Another tendency in generative grammar is to prefer "deep principles" over "ad hoc formulations", but formally this distinction does not make much sense. Given a generative theory (in the above sense) and a sufficiently expressive formalism, one can always reaxiomitize the grammar so that some facts are basic and others are derived as theorems. So, our methodology will be to above all get the facts right, and only when that is achieved worry about which constraints are deep principles, or axioms, and which are theorems.

Psycholinguistic responsibility We are interested in a theory of linguistic competence, so processing strategies are not directly relevant. But, if our model has any chance of being right, it must at least be compatible with what we know about the way language actually is processed. So, we can take a minimum position: a psychologically plausible grammar cannot depend irreducibly on computations that language users cannot possibly carry out.

Nondestructiveness A corollary to this (and to generativity) is that grammars should not make reference to operations that destroy existing structure. That is, they should be monotonic. Studies of human sentence processing suggest that language is processed incrementally, with syntactic, semantic, encyclopedic, and even frequency information being continuously integrated.

Locality This is another corollary: constraints should be local in the sense that whether a candidate satisfies the constraint can be determined by looking at that structure. There should not be any transderivational or transstructural constraints that require looking at other competing structures to determine the validity of a structure.

Parallelism Every grammatical theory makes reference to multiple levels of structure. In Government and Binding Theory, some levels (logical form, phonetic form) are derived from or read off of another level (S-structure). In constraint-based theories, on the other hand, all levels exist in parallel and are mutually constrained by the grammar. That is, if there are n levels, a linguistic expression is represented by an n-tuple of structures, with constraints potentially making reference to more than one level simultaneously.

Radical non-autonomy A corollary to this is that constraint-based theories of grammar do not take one level as primary. In particular, phrase structure is just one of many kinds of linguistic representation. Since all levels are represented in parallel, grammatical constraints may well constrain more than one level at once. Some constraints may happen to refer only to one level, but that is in no way the usual case.

None of Pollard's criteria are completely uncontroversial even within HPSG, and some (such as locality) have been explicitly rejected in other constraint-based frameworks. However, in general these goals characterize constraint-based theories of grammar as a class, and provide a methodological foundation for proceeding.

1.4 An outline of the theory

One of Pollard's more basic goals is to develop a theory in which what counts as a valid representation or rule can be given a formal characterization. In HPSG, the basic formal device used to represent everything is the typed feature structure.

As we saw above, the basic notation for a feature structure is the attribute value matrix, or AVM. We can think of an AVM as a description which picks out a set of satisfiers from a universe of abstract objects. These abstract objects correspond to linguistic objects, namely utterance types, and are what the linguistic theory is about. The theory itself is not made up of actual feature structures but of feature structure descriptions, which place constraints on the range of allowable utterance types.[1]

In addition to pairs of features and values, we assign each feature structure a type, where types group feature structures into classes. Types themselves are organized into an multiple-inheritance hierarchy which expresses subtype relations between types. The type hierarchy, along with appropriateness conditions which state what features an object of a given type may have, make up a type signature.

Using this metalanguage, we can start laying out the basic linguistic ontology we will need. First, the most basic linguistic unit is the *sign*, a pairing of a form with a meaning. Signs have two features, PHON and SYNSEM, corresponding to the two poles. At the coarsest level, we can divide signs into two kinds, *words* and *phrases*.

The lexicon consists of objects of type *word*, organized into a hierarchy of types and subtypes. Phrases differ from words in that they have internal structure and are built up out of smaller linguistic units (either words or other phrases). So, we can say that *phrases* have an additional feature DTRS, which takes as its value a list of signs. The inventory of constructions are all subtypes of the type *phrase*.

While signs are crucially bipolar structures made up of a *phon* and a *synsem* object, we will not have much to say about *phon* objects values in this study. We will assume that the value of the feature PHON is a list of phonological (or, more properly, orthographic) objects (for a more elaborated theory of phonological objects, see, e.g., Bird 1995 or Orgun 1996.)

1.4.1 X-bar theory

As presented by Pollard and Sag (1994), HPSG follows the familiar X-bar model. A handful of phrase structure schemata, including the three given in (6), define the set of valid tree structures.

(6) a. X → Subj, Head
                           [COMPS $\langle \, \rangle$]

   b. X → Head, Comps

   c. X → Spr, Head
                           [COMPS $\langle \, \rangle$]

In each phrase, categorial and selectional information is projected from the lexical entry of the head by a number of feature-passing conventions,

---

[1] Feature structures can be formalized in a number of alternative ways (e.g., Kaplan and Bresnan 1982, Carpenter 1992, King 1997, Richter 2000), but for the purposes of this discussion we will gloss over details of the underlying feature logic.

the most important of which are given in (7).

(7) a. Head Feature Principle

In a headed phrase, the HEAD value of the mother is token-identical to the HEAD value of the head daughter.

b. Valence Principle

For each valence feature F (one of SUBJ, SPR, and COMPS), the F value of the head daughter is the concatenation of the phrase's F value with the SYNSEMs of the F-DTRS.

The external distribution of a phrase is determined by its category, projected from the lexical head. This category projection is ensured by the Head Feature Principle, given in (7a). On the other hand, the Valence Principle, in (7b), controls valence satisfaction and valence cancellation and so determines what can occur as a sister to the head.

1.4.2 Construction types

The way of looking at phrase structure alluded to in §1.4.1 is very much in the spirit of conventional phrase structure grammars, but it is not the only way of approaching it. Roughly following Bouma et al. (in press), the basic feature architecture is given in (8):

(8)
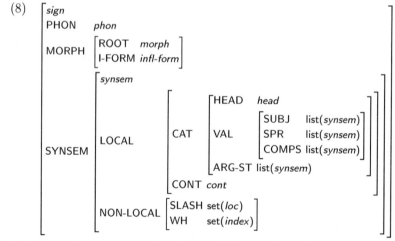

Each structure in square brackets is an AVM, a matrix of feature names and values. Feature names are in ALL CAPS and type names are in *italics*. The value of a feature can either be another AVM or it can be an atomic feature structure (indicated by a type name). The types list(α) and set(α) are parametric polymorphic types which represent a list of objects of type α and a set of objects of type α, respectively.

AVMs are used to represent all the information that a speaker might have about an utterance, and as a consequence they tend to grow quite large and difficult to read. To make them more compact, feature paths such as (9a) will be abbreviated as in (9b):

(9) a.
$$\left[\text{SYNSEM}\left[\text{LOCAL}\left[\text{CAT}\left[\text{VALENCE}\begin{bmatrix}\text{SUBJ} & \langle \textit{synsem}\rangle \\ \text{COMPS} & \langle \textit{synsem}\rangle\end{bmatrix}\right]\right]\right]\right]$$

  b.
$$\left[\text{SYNSEM} \mid \text{LOCAL} \mid \text{CAT} \mid \text{VALENCE}\begin{bmatrix}\text{SUBJ} & \langle \textit{synsem}\rangle \\ \text{COMPS} & \langle \textit{synsem}\rangle\end{bmatrix}\right]$$

Feature structures in HPSG are always well typed in the sense of Carpenter (1992). That means that every feature structure of some type only includes features that are appropriate for that type, and for each feature there is a unique type that it is appropriate for. Given a feature, one can always tell where it fits into the overall feature geometry. That means that (9b) can be unambiguously written as:

(10)
$$\begin{bmatrix}\text{SUBJ} & \langle \textit{synsem}\rangle \\ \text{COMPS} & \langle \textit{synsem}\rangle\end{bmatrix}$$

In what follows I will freely leave out features where doing so will not create undue confusion.

Considerable work in HPSG has focused on examining the hierarchical structure of the lexicon (e.g., Flickinger 1987, Zajac 1992, Riehemann 1998). More recently, building on the insights of Construction Grammar (Fillmore 1985, Fillmore et al. 1988, Goldberg 1995, Fillmore 1999, Kay and Fillmore 1999, Fillmore and Kay to appear), Sag (1997) has investigated applying the same methods of hierarchical classification to types of phrasal signs, or **constructions.** A relevant part of the basic classification of constructions corresponding to (6) and (7) is given in (11).

(11)

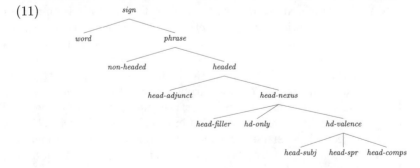

Phrases can be divided into two types: endocentric *headed* phrases and exocentric *non-headed* phrases. Since syntactic constraints are stated as constraints on particular types of signs, the Head Feature Principle (7a) can be represented as (12), a constraint on all signs of the type *headed*.

(12)   *headed* →

$$\begin{bmatrix} \text{HEAD} & \boxed{1} \\ \text{HD-DTR} & \begin{bmatrix} \text{HEAD} & \boxed{1} \end{bmatrix} \end{bmatrix}$$

This type constraint can be interpreted as an implication. Anything that is either of type *headed* or some more specific type must satisfy the given constraint. Boxed numbers, or tags, indicate structure sharing, so this constraint means that the HEAD value of a phrase is token-identical to the HEAD value of its head daughter.

Headed phrases are in turn divided into *head-adjunct* phrases and *head-nexus* phrases. Head-nexus phrases are phrases which discharge some grammatical dependency, either a subcategorization requirement (*valence*) or the SLASH value of an unbounded dependency construction (*head-filler*). Finally, *valence* phrases can be subtyped according to the kind of subcategorization dependency they discharge (subject, specifier, or complement).

In addition, constructions inherit constraints from the cross-cutting classification of phrases into either *clauses* or *non-clauses*. Among other things, clauses are subject to the following constraint:

(13)   *clause* →

$$\begin{bmatrix} \text{SYNSEM} \mid \text{LOCAL} & \begin{bmatrix} \text{CAT} \mid \text{VALENCE} \mid \text{SUBJ list}(\textit{non-canonical}) \\ \text{CONT } \textit{psoa} \end{bmatrix} \end{bmatrix}$$

This constraint states that the SUBJ list of a clause must be a list of zero or more *non-canonical* synsem objects. This ensures that either the clause contains an overt subject (and so the SUBJ list is empty) or the unexpressed subject (e.g., in control constructions) is either a *PRO* or a *gap*. *PRO* is a special type of synsem object that at minimum specifies accusative case and pronominal semantics (either *ppro* or *refl*) Note that this *PRO* is quite unlike the homonomous empty category of Chomsky and Lasnik (1977). Its purpose is only to put constraints on the ARG-ST of a verb in a control structure, and it does not correspond to a phonologically unrealized position in the phrase structure. *Gap* is a synsem object whose SLASH set contains its LOCAL value as a member. We will look at the role of *PRO* in more detail in §2.3.3. In addition, the constraint in (13) restricts the semantic type of a clause's content:

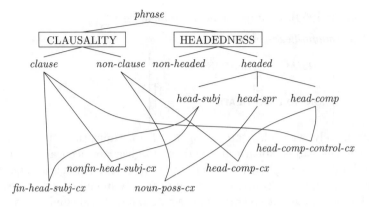

FIGURE 1   Some English construction types

the CONT value of a clause must be a *psoa* object (roughly speaking, an event).

These two hierarchies define a set of constraints on phrasal signs. These constraints constitute what Bloomfield (1933, 166) termed tagmemes, the "smallest meaningful units of grammatical form".[2] A **syntactic construction** is a meaningful recurrent bundle of tagmemes. One way to think of constructions is as the syntactic equivalent of what in the lexical domain would be called morphemes. In terms of the theory of phrasal types presented here, a construction is a phrasal sign type that inherits from both the *headedness* hierarchy and the *clausality* hierarchy. Since a construction licenses a type of complex sign, it must include information about how both the form and the meaning are assembled from the form and the meaning of its component parts. A construction may inherit some aspects of its meaning from its supertypes. In contrast to the strictly head-driven view of semantics presented by Pollard and Sag (1994), a construction may also have idiosyncratic meaning associated with it.

Some of the basic constructions of English are shown in Figure 1. The *fin-head-subj-cx* and the *nonfin-head-subj-cx* constructions combine a subcategorized-for subject with a finite and non-finite head, respectively. The finite version, for normal English sentences like *They walk* requires a nominative subject. The non-finite version, for 'minor' sentence types like absolutes (e.g., *With Pat running things, we're bound to succeed*) or 'Mad magazine' sentences (e.g., *What me worry?,* see

---

[2]This is one way in which the HPSG conception of constructions differs from, say, that of Zwicky (1994), for whom the building blocks of constructions are 'formal conditions' comparable to Bloomfield's **taxemes**.

Lambrecht 1990), requires an accusative subject.[3]

(14) *nonfin-head-subj-cx* →

$$
\begin{bmatrix}
\text{SYNSEM} & \begin{bmatrix} \text{HEAD} \begin{bmatrix} \text{ROOT } - \end{bmatrix} \end{bmatrix} \\
\text{NON-HD-DTR} & \begin{bmatrix} \text{HEAD} \begin{bmatrix} noun \\ \text{CASE } acc \end{bmatrix} \end{bmatrix}
\end{bmatrix}
$$

Alternatively, we could state as a general constraint that all NPs which are not the subject of a finite verb in English are accusative, an approach taken by Sag and Wasow (1999). This construction is also marked [ROOT −], and so is constrained to appear only in embedded contexts.

The *noun-poss-cx* construction (e.g., *Sandy's book*) combines a noun head with a possessive specifier to form a phrase with a *nom-obj* (i.e., an index bearing unit) as the CONTENT value. To be more precise, the construction type *noun-poss-cx* is subject to the following constraint:

(15) *noun-poss-cx* →

$$
\begin{bmatrix}
\text{SYNSEM} & \begin{bmatrix} \text{CAT | HEAD } noun \\ \text{CONT } nom\text{-}obj \end{bmatrix} \\
\text{NON-HD-DTR | SYNSEM | CAT | HEAD} & \begin{bmatrix} noun \\ \text{CASE } gen \end{bmatrix}
\end{bmatrix}
$$

Here for convenience I assume that the English genitive case marker *'s* is an edge inflection (Zwicky 1987, Halpern 1995). The two head-complement constructions both combine a head with its selected-for complements, but differ as to whether the resulting phrase can function as a clause. Unlike the *head-comp-cx* construction, *head-comp-control-cx* is a clause and so is subject to the constraint in (13).

1.4.3 Valence Principle

Given the view of phrase structure rules as constructions presented in §1.4.2, standard presentations of the Valence Principle (7b) contain an unneeded redundancy. Since the kind of valence requirement discharged by a phrase is represented as part of the type of the phrase, there is no need to distinguish SUBJ-DTRS, COMPS-DTRS and SPR-DTRS with different feature names, as in Pollard and Sag (1994).

Sag (1997) proposed an alternative formulation of the Valence Principle intended to eliminate this redundancy:

---

[3]Here and in what follows I assume that all constituents are binary branching. This assumption simplifies the constraints slightly, but nothing important rests on it. If it turns out to be necessary, things could be reformulated slightly to allow non-branching and/or multiple-branching structures.

(16)   *hd-ph* →

$$\begin{bmatrix} \text{SUBJ} & / \;\boxed{1} \\ \text{SPR} & / \;\boxed{2} \\ \text{COMPS} & / \;\boxed{3} \\ \text{HD-DTR} & \begin{bmatrix} \text{SUBJ} & / \;\boxed{1} \\ \text{SPR} & / \;\boxed{2} \\ \text{COMPS} & / \;\boxed{3} \end{bmatrix} \end{bmatrix}$$

Values marked with '/' are defaults. That is, they are soft constraints that can be overriden by a conflicting constraint on a more specific type. The role of defaults in the grammar will be considered in more depth in §3.4.2.

What (16) says is that the default condition is that a headed phrase has the same values for the valence features as the phrase's head daughter. Individual constructions types can override this default constraint to allow valence cancellation:[4]

(17)   *head-comp-ph* →

$$\begin{bmatrix} \text{COMPS} \;\boxed{1} \\ \text{HD-DTR} \,|\, \text{COMPS} \;\langle\,\boxed{2}\,|\,\boxed{1}\,\rangle \\ \text{NON-HD-DTR} \,|\, \text{SYNSEM} \;\boxed{2} \end{bmatrix}$$

The first element of the head daughter's COMPS list is $\boxed{2}$; $\boxed{1}$ is the list containing all but the first element of COMPS. The *head-comp-ph* construction produces a phrase whose COMPS value is the head daughter's COMPS value minus the non-head daughter's SYNSEM value. Since (17) has nothing to say about the SPR and SUBJ values, they get passed up from the head daughter by the default constraint in (16).

While this formalization of the Valence Principle produces the desired results, it treats valence cancellation as an idiosyncratic property of certain constructions and thus fails to capture the intuitive generalization underlying the Valence Principle. In particular, nothing about (16) would rule out a construction like the following:

(18)   *weird-head-comp-ph* →

$$\begin{bmatrix} \text{SPR} \;\boxed{1} \\ \text{HD-DTR} \,|\, \text{COMPS} \;\langle\,\boxed{2}\,|\,\boxed{1}\,\rangle \\ \text{NON-HD-DTR} \,|\, \text{SYNSEM} \;\boxed{2} \end{bmatrix}$$

---

[4]The notation $\langle X \,|\, Y \rangle$ denotes a list whose initial member is X and whose non-initial members make up the list Y.

This construction, like the construction in (17), combines a head with a complement. But in this case, the COMPS list of the whole phrase will be the same as the COMPS list of the head daughter, and the SPR value of the whole phrase will be the remainder of the COMPS list. If it is hard to see what that means, then the point is made: constructions like (18) do violence to our intuitions about specifiers, complements, and valence cancellation, and should be ruled out by a sufficiently general formulation of the Valence Principle.

The fact that unattested constructions can be described using the same formalism as HPSG is not by itself a problem. In fact, the HPSG formalism is completely general and is capable of representing many non-grammars (Carpenter 1991). One must distinguish between a linguistic formalism and linguistic theory. It is the role of a substantive theory of language to distinguish between valid and invalid linguistic representations within some formalism.

In this case, though, the failure of (16) to rule out constructions like (18) really is a problem. The constraint in (16) is supposed to be a formalization of the constraint stated informally in (7b). Since (7b) clearly rules out constructions like (18), the formalization in (16) must be too weak.

The following constraint captures the intuition behind the Valence Principle without requiring default inheritance and rules out bizarre construction types like (18):[5]

(19)　*headed* $\rightarrow$

$$
\begin{bmatrix}
\text{SYNSEM | CAT | VALENCE} \begin{bmatrix} \text{SUBJ} & \boxed{1} - \langle \boxed{2} \rangle \\ \text{SPR} & \boxed{3} - \langle \boxed{2} \rangle \\ \text{COMPS} & \boxed{4} - \langle \boxed{2} \rangle \end{bmatrix} \\
\text{HD-DTR | SYNSEM | CAT | VALENCE} \begin{bmatrix} \text{SUBJ} & \boxed{1} \\ \text{SPR} & \boxed{3} \\ \text{COMPS} & \boxed{4} \end{bmatrix} \\
\text{NON-HD-DTR | SYNSEM} \;\boxed{2}
\end{bmatrix}
$$

Individual constructions place constraints on the non-head daughter, but do not need to mention the valence of the mother:

(20)　*head-comp-ph* $\rightarrow$

$$
\begin{bmatrix}
\text{HD-DTR | COMPS} & \langle \boxed{5} \mid \boxed{6} \rangle \\
\text{NON-HD-DTR | SYNSEM} & \boxed{5}
\end{bmatrix}
$$

---

[5]We can define '$-$' in terms of Reape's (1994) domain union operator '$\bigcirc$': $X - Y = Z \leftrightarrow Y \bigcirc Z = X$.

This constraint ensures that undischarged valence requirements get propagated from the head of a phrase. In the case of, say, a head-modifier phrase, the non-head daughter ☐2 will not be a member of the SUBJ, SPR, or COMPS value of the head, and so the valence values will be passed up unchanged. In the case of, say, a head-complement phrase, ☐2 will be on the head's COMPS list ☐4, so the mother's COMPS value is the head's COMPS value minus the discharged complement.

1.4.4 Why HPSG?

Now that some of the technical machinery that I will be assuming in this study has been introduced, it is a good idea to question how much of it is really necessary for the analyses I will present. There are two aspects of HPSG that will turn out to be essential: its sign-based architecture and its reliance on type hierarchies. Other formal aspects of HPSG will be referred to in passing, for example in §2.3.4 where I will show how the pied piping properties of English verbal gerunds follow from Ginzburg and Sag's (1998) general treatment of interrogatives. However, any linguistic theory that covers a similar range of data should make the same predictions.

Since the only aspects of HPSG that are crucial to my argument are its orientation towards linguistic signs and its use of inheritance hierarchies, any grammatical theory that shared these properties of HPSG would work as well. One such theory is Construction Grammar (Fillmore and Kay to appear). In fact, HPSG and Construction Grammar have many features in common, and the variety of HPSG that I will be assuming here is heavily influenced by developments in Construction Grammar. So, I believe that whatever consequences the present work has for HPSG apply equal well to Construction Grammar.

Another grammatical framework that is similar to HPSG in the relevant respects is Cognitive Grammar (Langacker 1987a). Cognitive Grammar (CG) and HPSG are less obviously alike in other respects, but I want to argue that they are fundamentally compatible and that the differences between the frameworks are not as profound as they might at first appear.

The most obvious difference between the two frameworks is in their notation. The metalanguage used to describe HPSG is based on logical notations, while CG is couched in a spatially-oriented diagrammatic notation that is meant to be interpreted intuitively. However, the two metalanguages encode essentially the same information. For example, compare the HPSG and the CG representations for the content of the phrase *on the mat* in Figure 2 and Figure 3, respectively. In both cases, the contribution of the definite article *the* has been ignored.

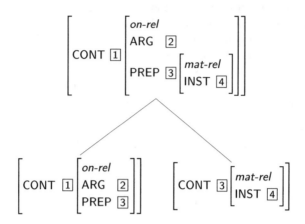

FIGURE 2 HPSG representation of *on the mat*

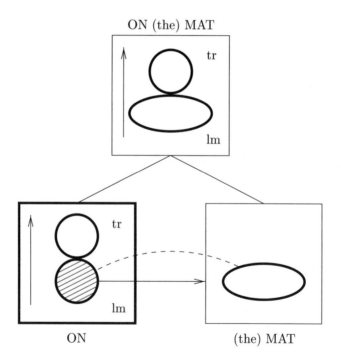

FIGURE 3 CG representation of *on the mat* (van Hoek 1997, 22)

In both cases, the meaning of *on* is represented as a relation between two other representations. In HPSG, that relation is named *on-rel*, while in CG it is named ↑. The two things that stand in the ↑ relation are called the TRAJECTOR (tr) and the LANDMARK (lm), while the two things in the *on-rel* relation are (for no particular reason) called the ARG and the PREP. In both cases, the meaning of the whole phrase is determined by the meaning of the left daughter, elaborated in a specific way by the meaning of the right daughter. So, while on the surface the two representations look radically different, they actually contain the same information.

An apparently more substantive difference between the two frameworks is the position each takes towards the role of syntactic constraints. In both frameworks, the basic level of representation is the sign, a form/content pair. In HPSG, the sign also contains purely syntactic constraints. In contrast, CG explicitly denies the existence of any purely syntactic information (Langacker 1987a, 53f):

> ... the only structures permitted in the grammar of a language (or among the substantive specifications of universal grammar) are (1) phonological, semantic, or symbolic structures that actually occur in linguistic expressions; (2) schemas for such structures; and (3) categorizing relationships involving the elements in (1) and (2). Hence no descriptive constructs are permitted that lack both phonological and semantic content.

Since most of the information in an HPSG sign like (8) is neither phonological nor semantic, this would seem to be a fundamental difference between the frameworks. However, I think if one looks at the information actually represented in each framework, this difference turns on terminology more than anything else.

Head-complement constructs are licensed by the head-complement construction in HPSG and by the head-complement schema in CG. Simplified versions of the constraints on each are given in Figures 4 and 5. In Figure 5, each sign is a pair of boxes. The upper box is the phonology and the lower box is the semantics. The schema controls how these parts of the component signs contribute to the composite expression. The constraints in Figure 4 do the same thing, but they also refer to two additional pieces of information not found in the CG structure, namely the values of COMPS and HEAD.

If we consider what these features are doing, however, it is clear that the same information must be represented covertly in Figure 5. The feature COMPS tells us whether a particular sign can function as the left

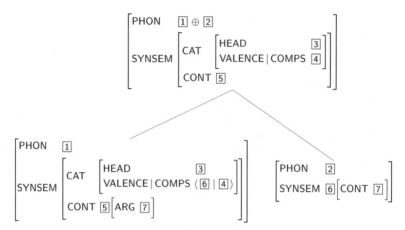

FIGURE 4 Head-complement construction

daughter in a head-complement construction and, if it can, what kind of sign can occur as the right daughter along with it. In CG that kind of combinatorial information is not represented as part of the sign, but instead is built into the definition of the construction. It is assumed that valence is largely predictable from semantic type, i.e., that correctly specifying the content of the left and right daughters in Figure 5 will predict the majority of head-complement combinations. Any head-complement combinations that do not follow from some semantic (or phonological) principle are listed as exceptional construction schemas. A similar case can be made for the value of HEAD.

So the real difference between HPSG and CG here is not whether syntax 'exists', but is in the way syntax is represented. For HPSG, the assumption is that valence relations are not generally predictable on the basis of meaning, but when they are the relevant generalizations can be stated as constraints in the lexical hierarchy (see §3.4.1). For CG, the assumption is that valence relations are predictable from meaning, but when they are not, the relevant exceptions can be stated as specialized schemas. Either way, the bottom line is that the same information is being expressed.[6]

This is not to say that HPSG and CG are in any way equivalent. There are deep foundational differences between the two frameworks, and analyses of particular phenomena in the two frameworks are often

[6]Interestingly, some efforts by computational linguists to convert HPSG grammars into a form that allows more efficient processing have yielded grammars that look a lot like those posited by CG (e.g., Neumann 1994).

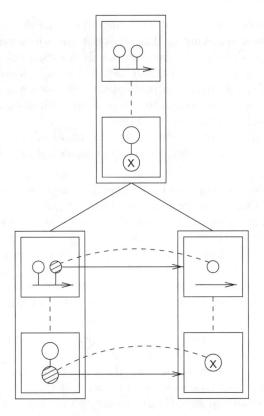

FIGURE 5 Head-complement schema (adapted from van Hoek 1997, 26)

quite different (cf. Pollard and Sag 1994 and van Hoek 1997 on binding theory). All I want to claim here is that the frameworks are not incommensurable and in fact are more alike than has often been assumed. Because of their similarity, there is the potential for a fruitful dialogue between the frameworks. One small goal of the current study is to show how notions from cognitive and functional approaches to language can shed light on the problems traditionally considered by formal linguists and, hopefully, that the converse is also true.

1.5 Universals in HPSG

The question of linguistic universals has not been a central area of inquiry in most HPSG research. Instead, the focus has been on detailed description and analysis of particular languages. This is in stark contrast to most formally oriented theories of grammar, for which the search for universals is the primary goal, with linguistic description being merely one step toward achieving it. This does not mean however that it is in principle impossible to talk about universals in HPSG, only that it is not necessary. Indeed, it is standardly assumed that at least some of the properties of the grammars of particular languages are shared with the grammars of other languages. In this section, I will discuss two sources for this commonality among languages.

One exception to this absence of work on universals in HPSG is Ackerman and Webelhuth's (1998) theory of grammatical archetypes.[7] They point out:

> In our estimation, two facts about language need to be accounted for by an explanatory theory of grammar. On the one hand there *are* linguistic structures that seem to reappear systematically in the world's languages with greater than chance frequency... On the other hand, an explanatory theory of grammar should also be capable of allowing for purely language-particular structures that seem to be the result of unusual diachronic developments and hence don't recur systematically in other languages. (129)

They go on to argue that neither Chomsky's nativist approach nor the purely empiricist approach of Rumelhart and McClelland (1986) have been able to adequately account for these two facts. Instead, they propose that Universal Grammar provides a set of types organized into a hierarchy that any language is free to incorporate into its own type hierarchy, by what they call archetype activation. The activation of less marked archetypes imposes less of a "markedness cost" on a language than activation of more marked archetypes, so less marked archetypes will be found more frequently across languages and in a wider variety of languages. However, the grammar of each language is unique, and while it is shaped in part by the choices made available by Universal Grammar, it also reflects the unique history of that language. Language particular types incur the greatest markedness cost and therefore are found less frequently. In §3.4, I will show how the universal properties of mixed categories arise through the interaction of the universal categorial archetypes, and in §4.2.1 I will consider some of the possible origins of grammatical archetypes.

Universal archetypes provide one source for regularities across languages. However, there are more general organizing principles that also give rise to cross-linguistic uniformity. If the inventory of types in the grammar of a particular language is largely governed by the marked-

---

[7]A similar model is hinted at but not fully developed by Kay (1994).

ness of archetype activation, then the organization of those types into a parochial hierarchy is governed by the principle of motivation.

Many constructions have properties that are not fully predictable and yet are also not completely arbitrary. We can say that such signs are *motivated*. The standard example of motivation, due to Saussure (1916), is the contrast between French *vingt* 'twenty' and *dix-neuf* 'nineteen'. Both are arbitrary associations of form and meaning, but unlike *vingt*, *dix-neuf* "suggests its own terms and other terms associated with it (e.g., *dix* 'ten', *neuf* 'nine', *vingt-neuf* 'twenty-nine', *dix-huit* 'eighteen', *soixante-dix* 'seventy', etc.)" (131). Given the linguistic system that it is embedded in (i.e., the grammar of French), the pairing of the form *dix-neuf* with the meaning 'nineteen' is not surprising, even if it is not strictly predictable. Likewise, while the properties of mixed categories are not strictly predictable, they are not surprising given the properties of more prototypical nouns and verbs. Any analysis of mixed categories like verbal gerunds should be able to show they fit into the language's overall system of categories.

In addition to allowing generalizations to be expressed, the type hierarchy also provides a natural characterization of motivation. In Construction Grammar, default inheritance is used to give a formal characterization of such system-internal motivation: "A given construction is *motivated* to the degree that its structure is inherited from other constructions in the language... An optimal system is a system that maximizes motivation" (Goldberg 1995, 70). Thus, the type hierarchy reflects the way in which constructions are influenced by their relationships with other constructions within the language and allows what Lakoff (1987) calls the "ecological niche" of a construction within a language to be captured as part of the formal system.

2

English Verbal Gerunds

2.1 Properties of verbal gerunds

Quirk et al. (1985, 1290) describe a number of English nominalization strategies, a few of which are demonstrated in (1).

(1) a. *Brown's painting of his daughter* hangs in the town museum.
    b. *The painting of Brown* is as skillful as that of Gainsborough.
    c. *Brown's deft painting of his daughter* is a delight to watch.
    d. *Brown's deftly painting his daughter* is a delight to watch.
    e. Brown is well known for *painting his daughter.*
    f. I dislike *Brown painting his daughter.*
    g. Brown *is painting* his daughter.

As these examples show, the uses of words in *-ing* fall along an apparent continuum that ranges from fully noun-like uses to fully verb-like uses. The uses that this section is concerned with, the verbal gerunds, are the intermediate cases in (1d–f). Verbal gerunds do not have all the characteristics of either nouns or verbs, but seem to fall somewhere in between these two categories. In this section, I will review some of the nominal and verbal characteristics of verbal gerunds as they have been described in the literature (primarily Abney 1987 and Pullum 1991) and the problems they pose for traditional parts of speech.

2.1.1 Verbal gerunds as nouns

The strongest evidence for the nominal nature of verbal gerunds comes from the external distribution of verbal gerund phrases (VGerPs). Like NPs, VGerPs can appear in argument positions:

(2) a. Pat('s) getting arrested alarmed Chris.
    b. Chris witnessed Pat('s) getting arrested.

In addition, VGerPs appear in contexts where otherwise only NPs can occur. For one, declarative clauses, unlike NPs, are generally prohibited from occurring sentence internally (Ross 1967, Kuno 1973):[1]

(3) a. *I believe that Pat took a leave of absence bothers you.
     b. *Why does that Pat took a leave of absence bother you?
     c. *It's that Pat took a leave of absence that bothers you.

However, VGerPs are subject to no such constraint:

(4) a. I believe that Pat('s) taking a leave of absence bothers you.
     b. Why does Pat('s) taking a leave of absence bother you?
     c. It's Pat('s) taking a leave of absence that bothers you.

This is a point about which there has been some disagreement in the literature. Reuland (1983), for instance, claims that accusative subject VGerPs cannot appear clause internally. However, consider the following examples:

(5) a. *Did that Pat got arrested bother you?
     b. *Did for Pat to get arrested bother you?
     c. *Did to get arrested bother you?
     d. ?Did Pat getting arrested bother you?
     e. Did getting arrested bother you?
     f. Did Pat's getting arrested bother you?
     g. Did Pat's arrest bother you?

While (5d) may be somewhat awkward, there is a clear difference in acceptability between (5a–c) on the one hand and (5d–g) on the other. Therefore it is reasonable to conclude that with respect to the prohibition against sentence-internal clausal arguments, VGerPs behave like NPs and not like Ss.

Similarly, VGerPs can occur as the object of a preposition, a position Ss are normally barred from:

(6) a. Pat is concerned about Sandy('s) getting arrested.
     b. *Pat is concerned about (that) Sandy got arrested.

One thing worth pointing out here is that verbal gerund phrases do not have the full distribution of NPs. In particular, as we see in (7) verbal gerunds cannot happily be possessive specifiers.

(7) a. Pat's leave of absence's bothering you surprises me.
     b. *Pat's/Pat taking a leave of absence's bothering you surprises me.
     c. *That Pat took a leave of absence's bothering you surprised me.

---

[1]Some speakers find starred the examples in (3) and (5) awkward but not ungrammatical. For those speakers the constraint against sentence internal clauses is apparently not an absolute prohibition.

In this case, VGerPs seem to behave more like Ss and less like NPs. But, as Zwicky and Pullum (1996) observed, only a restricted subclass of what are otherwise clearly NPs can show up as possessives, for example, *this Tuesday* in (8).

(8) a. This Tuesday is a good day for me.
     b. *this Tuesday's being a good day for me

In other contexts, though, these examples do not sound as bad:

(9) a. Did you go to this Tuesday's lecture?
     b. ?Pat's taking a leave of absence's impact will be considerable

So, this suggests that verbal gerunds, like the other cases described by Zwicky and Pullum, fall into a "functionally restricted" subclass of nouns that only marginally head possessive phrases.

What makes these particular NPs exceptional may well be their semantics. Prototypical NPs denote objects, whether physical or abstract. In contrast, the NP *this Tuesday* denotes a temporal location, and can even by used adverbially to modify a VP:

(10)   Pat is flying to Bolivia this Tuesday.

Likewise, verbal gerund phrases denote an event. As Taylor (1995, 193) puts it, "the ease with which nouns can designate a 'possessor' appears to correlate with the closeness to the *semantically* defined prototype."

On the other side of things, there are contexts which admit verbal gerunds but not regular NPs. Jørgensen (1981) and Quirk et al. (1985, 1230) discuss a class of predicative heads which select for an expletive subject and a verbal gerund complement, as in (11).

(11)   There's no use (you/your) telling him anything.

The fact that the complement's subject can appear in the possessive shows that the complement really is a verbal gerund phrase and that this is not a case of subject-to-object raising. Examples such as this provide evidence that verbal gerunds form a subcategory of noun distinct from common nouns.

2.1.2 Verbal gerunds as verbs

While the external syntax of verbal gerunds is much like that of NPs, their internal structure is more like that of VPs. For one, verbal gerunds take adverbial modifiers. In contrast, true nouns take adjectival modifiers:

(12) a. Pat disapproved of (me/my) *quiet/quietly leaving before anyone noticed.
     b. Pat disapproved of my quiet/*quietly departure.

    c. The careful/*carefully restoration of the painting took six months.

Similarly, verbal gerunds can be negated with the particle *not*. But, *not* cannot be used to negate a noun:[2]

(13) a. Pat's not having bathed for a week disturbed the other diners.

      b. *The not processing of the election results created a scandal.

Also, verbal gerunds take accusative NP complements, while the nominal gerund in (14b) can only take a PP complement:

(14) a. (Pat's/Pat) diligently calling (*of) the roll started each day.

      b. The diligent calling *(of) the roll started each day.

These facts have been used to motivate the claim that verbal gerunds must be verbs at some level (e.g., Abney 1987). However, none of the behavior exhibited in (12)–(14) is unique to verbs. Some of the verb-like properties of gerunds are also shared by prepositions and adjectives. Adverbials can modify prepositions and adjectives as well as verbal gerunds and verbs, while common nouns take adjectival modifiers:

(15) a. Sandy rarely gets enough sleep.

      b. Sandy lives directly beneath a dance studio.

      c. Sandy's apartment has an insufficiently thick ceiling.

      d. Sandy grumbles about the dancers' nocturnally rehearsing *Swan Lake*.

      e. Sandy's repeated(*ly) complaint brought no satisfaction.

Similarly, *not* can be used in some circumstances to negate adverbs, adjectives, PPs, and determiners:

(16) a. Not surprisingly, the defendant took the Fifth.

      b. The conference will be held in Saarbrücken, not far from the French border.

      c. Not many people who have gone over Niagara Falls live to tell about it.

These facts about modification and negation do not show that verbal gerunds are verbs. What they show is that verbal gerunds, unlike common nouns, are part of a larger class of expressions which includes verbs.

---

[2]The only exception is in the *not...but* correlative coordination construction, which admits NPs but does not admit N's:

(i)   Employees wore identification badges listing not only their names but also their dates of hire.

(ii) *Employees wore identification badges listing their not only names but also dates of hire.

The complementation facts also do not constitute a strong argument that verbal gerunds must be verbs. Verbs, prepositions and verbal gerunds, unlike common nouns and adjectives, can take NP complements:

(17) a. Robin sees the house.
    b. Robin searched behind the house.
    c. Robin's watching the house unnerved the tenants.
    d. Robin's surveillance *(of) the house was illegal.

On the other hand, some verbs only take PP complements:

(18) a. *The strike extended two weeks.
    b. The strike extended through the summer.

In addition, common nouns do occur with accusative complements in other Indo-European languages (see Dal 1952). What these examples show is that taking adverbial modifiers and NP complements are neither necessary nor sufficient conditions for verbhood. The fact that some verbal gerunds take accusative objects is therefore not especially significant.

What is important to note is that a verbal gerund, unlike a nominal gerund, takes the same complements as the corresponding main verb:

(19) a. Chris casually put the roast in the oven.
    b. Chris's/Chris casually putting the roast in the oven appalled the visiting vegetarians.
    c. Chris's casual putting of the roast in the oven appalled the visiting vegetarians.

This extends even to derived subcategorization frames, such as the passive or the resultative:

(20) a. Pat was helped by Sandy.
    b. Pat's being helped by Sandy made all the difference.
    c. Lee hammered the sheet flat.
    d. Lee's hammering the sheet flat made a terrible noise.

So, what we can say is that a VGerP headed by the *-ing* form of a verb has the same internal distribution as a VP headed by a finite form of that same verb.

2.1.3 Subtypes of verbal gerund phrases

To summarize, VGerPs have four basic properties that need to be accounted for:

(21) a. A verbal gerund takes the same complements as the verb from which it is derived.

    b. Verbal gerunds are modified by adverbs and not by adjectives.

    c. The entire verbal gerund phrase has the external distribution of an NP.

    d. The subject of the gerund is optional and, if present, can be either a genitive or an accusative NP.

The properties in (21a–c) are shared by accusative subject (ACC-*ing*), genitive subject (POSS-*ing*), and subjectless (PRO-*ing*) verbal gerund phrases and are not shared by any other English constructions. The three types of verbal gerunds seem to be subtypes of a single common construction type, and any analysis of verbal gerunds ought to be able to account for their similarities in a systematic way.

    It is important to note, however, that there are differences among the three types which also must be accounted for (Reuland 1983, Abney 1987). Of course, the most obvious difference is the case of the subject. In that respect, POSS-*ing* VGerPs are more like NPs, while ACC-*ing* VGerPs are more like Ss. In the next sections we will look at some of the less obvious differences.

2.1.3.1 Coordination

One possible difference between the ACC-*ing* and POSS-*ing* VGerPs discussed by Horn (1975) can be found in their agreement behavior when conjoined:

(22) a. That Pat came and that Chris left bothers/?bother me.

      b. Pat coming (so often) and Chris leaving (so often) bothers/??bother me.

      c. Coming (so often) and leaving (so often) bothers/??bother me.

      d. Pat's coming and Chris's leaving ??bothers/bother me.

      e. Pat and Chris *bothers/bother me.

Conjoined ACC-*ing* or PRO-*ing* VGerPs, like conjoined Ss, tend to trigger singular (or default) number agreement on the verb. Conjoined POSS-*ing* VGerPs, like conjoined nouns, trigger plural agreement. Furthermore, the two types of verbal gerunds cannot be comfortably conjoined:

(23) a. *Pat's coming and Chris leaving bothers/bother me.

      b. *Pat coming and Chris's leaving bothers/bother me.

The patterns of compatibility in (22) and (23) follow naturally from the assumption that ACC-*ing* and POSS-*ing* VGerP are of different semantic types. POSS-*ing* verbal gerund phrases, like noun phrases, have nominal semantics, with an index specified for person, number, and gender. In contrast, ACC-*ing* VGerPs, like Ss, have propositional semantics.

On the other hand, Portner (1992) calls into question the data in (22). He suggests that the behavior of conjoined VGerPs follows from "a tendency to interpret conjoined ACC-*ing*'s as describing a single event but to consider conjoined POSS-*ing*'s to describe different events" (112). When the specific meanings of the conjoined elements work against this tendency, as in (24), then agreement facts seems less clear:

(24) a. Pat swimming the English channel and Chris sailing around the world bother me.

  b. Pat's coming and Chris's consequently leaving bothers me.

Portner concludes that the examples in (22)–(24) do not point to a syntactic difference between ACC-*ing* and POSS-*ing* VGerPs, but that "agreement with gerunds is based on semantic factors" (113).

Further evidence for Portner's claim comes from the fact that this same problem arises with simple conjoined NPs. In (25), the subject can be interpreted either as a single individual (triggering singular agreement) or as two separate individuals (triggering plural agreement).

(25) Pat's brother and Chris's uncle is/are arriving tomorrow.

But, when *both* is prefixed to the subject, only the plural reading is possible:

(26) a. Both Pat's brother and Chris's uncle *is/are arriving tomorrow.

  b. Both Pat coming and Chris leaving *bothers/bother me.

The addition of *both* in (26b) reverses the contrast seen in (22b). This is true for conjoined VGerPs as well. So it seems that these coordination facts are part of a more general phenomenon and do not help us distinguish between ACC-*ing* and POSS-*ing* gerunds.

2.1.3.2 Quantifier scope

Another difference that Abney (1987) discusses relates to the scope possibilities for quantified subjects of verbal gerunds. A quantified expression in the subject of a POSS-*ing* VGerP can take wide scope, while a quantified expression in the subject of an ACC-*ing* VGerP cannot:[3]

(27) a. Someone talked about every team's appearing on television.
$\exists x \forall y$ talk-about$'(x, \text{appear-on-tv}'(y))$
$\forall y \exists x$ talk-about$'(x, \text{appear-on-tv}'(y))$

---

[3] *Every team appearing on television* can take wide scope in (27b) under the alternative and irrelevant reading in which *appearing on television* is a reduced relative clause modifying *team*.

b. Someone talked about every team appearing on television.
$\exists x \forall y$ talk-about$'(x,$ appear-on-tv$'(y))$

The same contrast can be seen between NPs and Ss:

(28) a. Someone talked about every team's television appearance.
$\exists x \forall y$ talk-about$'(x,$ appear-on-tv$'(y))$
$\forall y \exists x$ talk-about$'(x,$ appear-on-tv$'(y))$

   b. Someone talked about when every team appeared on television.
$\exists x \forall y$ talk-about$'(x,$ appear-on-tv$'(y))$

So, quantifier scope potential offers another piece of evidence that ACC-*ing* VGerPs are somehow clause-like, while POSS-*ing* VGerPs are somehow NP-like.

In contrast, Portner (1992) uses a different kind of operator scope potential to argue against the view that ACC-*ing* VGerPs are clauses at some level. He observes that while the scope of *not* is sometimes ambiguous in clauses, it is never ambiguous in VGerPs. For example, (29a) has two readings while (29b) allegedly has only one.

(29) a. Pat is not happy for five minutes each day.
¬for-five-minutes-each-day$'($happy$'($Pat$'))$
for-five-minutes-each-day$'($¬happy$'($Pat$'))$

   b. Pat('s) not being happy for five minutes each day...
for-five-minutes-each-day$'($¬happy$'($Pat$'))$

If ACC-*ing* VGerPs are really clauses, one might expect them to show the same scope ambiguities as clauses. Portner attributes the ambiguities seen in the clausal example to the presence of an I(nfl) node:

> In the derivation of [(29a)], *be* raises from within its VP projection to I. Assuming that both *not* and *for five minutes each day* are adjoined to VP, this will result in the word order seen in [(29a)] as well as a scope ambiguity—based on which is adjoined c-commanding the other—between the negation and the temporal. If the gerund in [(29b)] had the internal structure of clauses... there is no reason why its *be* should not be able to undergo the same operation. (94)

So, he concludes, neither ACC-*ing* nor POSS-*ing* VGerPs are nominal clauses and therefore the difference between the two types must be purely semantic.

One problem with this line of reasoning is empirical. It is not at all clear that negation cannot have wide scope over an adverbial within a VGerP. For example, if we replace the temporal adjunct in (29b) with one containing a quantifier or the negative polarity item *any,* we can encourage a reading in which *not* has wide scope:

(30) a. The President('s) not speaking in every city on the tour offended several mayors.

b. Pat('s) not being happy at any time is a cause for concern.

So, it appears that both kinds of VGerPs allow both scope readings. This might still be a problem for an analysis that depends on ACC-*ing* VGerPs being clausal and POSS-*ing* VGerPs being non-clausal. Following Portner's logic, this might be used to argue that *all* VGerPs are clausal. However, contrary to the presupposition of this argument, the non-clausal structure ultimately adopted by Portner (1992, 96) appear to allow both scope readings. Adapting Abney (1987), Portner assumes that VGerPs are headed by a phonetically null noun *ING* which selects for a VP[+ing] complement. The subject of the gerund (whether genitive or accusative) appears as the specifier of *ING*. As the structures in Figure 6 demonstrate, this allows gerunds to show exactly the same structural ambiguity between VP adjuncts as finite clauses show. So, the conclusion to reach is that the evidence in (29) has no bearing on the question of whether some gerunds are nominal clauses.

Portner's second argument against a clausal analysis of ACC-*ing* VGerPs based on quantifier scope is potentially more compelling. Portner observes another contrast between clauses and ACC-*ing* VGerPs (and non-contrast between ACC-*ing* and POSS-*ing* VGerPs):

(31) a. Everyone did not smile.
$\neg\forall x \text{ smile}'(x)$
$\forall x \neg\text{smile}'(x)$

b. Everyone('s) not smiling [...bothered Pat.]
$\forall x \neg\text{smile}'(x)$

In a finite clause with both the negative particle *not* and a quantifier like *every,* either logical operator can take wide scope over the other. However, in parallel examples of VGerPs, only the quantifier can take wide scope. Portner is somewhat unclear on how the derivation in (31a) works, but he assumes that the reading with wide scope negation crucially depends on the presence of an IP. Either *not* raises at LF to adjoin to IP or *everyone* lowers (via reconstruction) from [Spec, IP] back into the VP and below negation. Since (31b) is not ambiguous regardless of the case of the subject, he concludes that gerunds never have an I node and are never clausal.

Portner's argument is valid, given his assumptions about the syntax of negation. However, recent lexical analyses of English negation (Kim

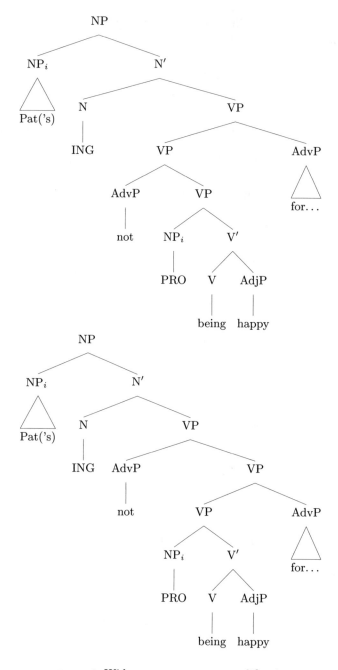

FIGURE 6 Wide vs. narrow scope modification

1995a, Kim and Sag 1995, Kim 1995b) offer an alternative account for the ambiguity of (31a) that does not entail Portner's conclusion. Kim and Sag argue that there are two *nots* in English. One is an adverb that negates the non-finite constituent that it appears to the left of, while the other is introduced by lexical rule as a complement of a finite auxiliary verb and negates the whole clause. This is the source of the ambiguity in (31a). Kim and Sag propose the following two structures for (31a):

(32) a.

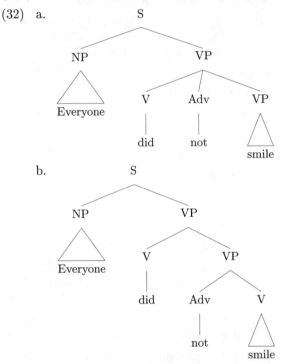

b.

In (32a), *not* is a complement of *did* and has scope over the entire clause, *not* is adjoined to *smile* and has scope only over the lower VP. In (29b) and (31b), on the other hand, there is no finite auxiliary and only the adverbial *not* can occur. Kim and Sag further argue that this lexical analysis can better account for the properties of English negation and for the differences between English and French than can Pollock's (1989) head movement analysis. So, given Kim and Sag's well-motivated analysis of negation, the absence of ambiguity in these gerund examples suggests that they are non-finite but tells us nothing about whether they are clauses.

2.1.3.3 Extraction

Another difference between the two type of VGerPs, first observed by Horn (1975), is that it seems to be possible to extract a complement from an ACC-*ing* VGerP but not from a genitive subject VGerP. The examples typically cited to show this are given in (33).

(33)　a.　Which city do you remember him describing?
　　　　b.　*Which city do you remember his describing?

While (33b) is typically reported as ungrammatical in the literature (e.g., Abney 1987), seemingly parallel examples do not show as strong a difference between ACC-*ing* and POSS-*ing* VGerPs:

(34)　a.　Which statue did you photograph him dedicating?
　　　　b.　?Which statue did you photograph his dedicating?

Following Portner (1992, 107ff), I would attribute the slight awkwardness of (34b) to specificity effects and the different presuppositions of the two types of VGerPs. Portner argues that POSS-*ing* gerunds are presupposed and therefore comparable to definite NPs, while ACC-*ing* gerunds are indefinite. For example, (35a) carries a presupposition that "there is an [event], perhaps only hypothetical, under discussion" (111). On the other hand, the ACC-*ing* gerund in (35b) is "lacking even this type of familiarity presupposition".

(35)　a.　Pat didn't want to discuss Sandy's coming to visit
　　　　b.　Pat didn't want to discuss Sandy coming to visit.

Portner further argues that this factivity/definiteness property of POSS-*ing* gerunds accounts for the following difference:

(36)　a.　Joyce usually dreams about Mary shouting at her.
　　　　b.　Joyce usually dreams about Mary's shouting at her.

In (36b) the gerund phrase can have a quantificational reading, while in (36a) it cannot. That is, (36b) has a reading which can be paraphrased as "most times Mary shouts at Joyce, Joyce dreams about it," while this reading is unavailable for (36b). This difference is also highlighted by the contrast in (37).

(37)　a.??Joyce usually dreams the next night about Mary shouting at her.
　　　　b.　Joyce usually dreams the next night about Mary's shouting at her.

Portner claims that the difference in (36) is parallel to the difference in (38):

(38)　a.　Pat always knows who won a prize.

b. Pat always wonders who won a prize.

Here, "because *know* presupposes the content of its complement ... a process of presupposition accommodation will make the open sentence *X won a prize* available to serve as the restrictive clause of the quantifier *always*" (108). Thus Portner argues that there is a connection between definiteness and the availability of adverbial quantification.

So, if POSS-*ing* gerunds are definite and ACC-*ing* gerunds are indefinite, this provides an immediate account of the contrasts in (33) and (34). As has long been recognized (Erteschik-Shir 1973), extraction from a definite NP is much worse than extraction from an indefinite NP:

(39) a. Who did you see a picture of?
b. *Who did you see the picture of?

Fiengo and Higginbotham (1981) attribute this contrast to a specificity condition, which Diesing (1992, 103) revises as the following descriptive generalization:

(40) Presuppositional NP Constraint
Extraction cannot take place out of a presuppositional NP.

Questions remain about what exactly constitutes a "presuppositional NP", and many of the grammaticality judgements cited in this section are quite fragile. But, if Portner is right about the presuppositional difference between ACC-*ing* and POSS-*ing* VGerPs, then the oddness of (33b) and (34b) can be subsumed under a more general constraint. So, the conclusion is that there is no specific prohibition against extracting the complements of any kind of VGerPs, but that other constraints in the grammar may rule out particular examples.

2.1.3.4 Pied piping

Another difference between the two types of VGerPs, pointed out by Abney (1987), is that POSS-*ing* but not ACC-*ing* VGerPs with *WH* subjects can front under 'pied piping' (Ross 1967) in restrictive relative clauses:

(41) a. The person whose being late every day Pat didn't like got promoted anyway.
b. *The person who(m) being late every day Pat didn't like got promoted anyway.

Again, the same contrast can be seen between NPs and Ss:

(42) a. The person whose chronic lateness Pat didn't like got promoted anyway.
b. *The person (for) who(m) to be late every day Pat didn't like got promoted anyway.

The same generalization holds for *WH* questions:

(43) a. I wonder whose being late every day Pat didn't like?
b. *I wonder who(m) being late every day Pat didn't like?

(44) a. I wonder whose lateness Pat didn't like?
b. *I wonder (for) who(m) to be late every day Pat didn't like?

POSS-*ing* VGerPs, like NPs, can appear as the leftmost constituent of a *WH* question, while ACC-*ing* VGerPs, like clauses, cannot.

Curiously, Webelhuth (1992, 133ff) (drawing on Williams 1975) reports a different pattern of grammaticality than I am claiming here. He cites the following examples (with the given judgements):

(45) a. The administration objected to Bill's frequent travels to Chicago on financial grounds.
b. The administration objected to Bill's frequently traveling to Chicago on financial grounds.

(46) a. Whose frequent travels to Chicago did the administration object to on financial grounds?
b. *Whose frequently traveling to Chicago did the administration object to on financial grounds?

I am not sure I would agree that (46b) is strictly speaking ungrammatical. While it is certainly less felicitous than (46a), it is unquestionably much better than (47).

(47) *Who(m) frequently traveling to Chicago did the administration object to on financial grounds?

The question remains, though, why (46a) should be even slightly better than (46b). Part of the reason might be that this use of *traveling* is partially blocked by the existing and more or less synonymous *travel*, much like *curiosity* partially blocks the derivation of *?curiousness* (Aronoff 1976, Briscoe et al. 1995). When we change (46) to use a verb that has no common nominalized form, the contrast weakens even further:

(48) a. Whose frequent absences from Chicago did the administration object to on financial grounds?
b. Whose frequently leaving Chicago did the administration object to on financial grounds?

Why this blocking effect should be felt more strongly in (46) than in (45) is unclear, but it seems at least plausible that the source of the contrast in (46) is not due specifically to a constraint on pied piping.

While some (e.g., Abney 1987) have taken the contrast in (41) as another piece of evidence that ACC-*ing* VGerPs are clauses, Portner (1992) argues against this conclusion by pointing out that ACC-*ing* examples like (41b) and (43b) without pied piping are just as bad:

(49)   a. *The person who(m) Pat didn't like being late every day got promoted anyway.
       b. *I wonder who(m) Pat didn't like being late every day?

So, he concludes that the ungrammaticality of (41b) has nothing to do with restrictions on pied piping but that the best generalization to account for this data is that "ACC-*ing*'s are generally impossible with subject *WH*'s" (116). However, this generalization falsely predicts that ACC-*ing* VGerPs with *WH* subjects should be ungrammatical even in constructions which allow clauses with *WH* subjects. One such construction is the multiple *WH* question:

(50)   a. Pat wonders who didn't like whose chronic lateness.
       b. Pat wonders who didn't like (for) who(m) to be late every day.

ACC-*ing* VGerPs, like clauses, can in fact occur with *WH* subjects in multiple *WH* questions:

(51)   a. Pat wonders who didn't like whose being late every day.
       b. Pat wonders who didn't like who(m) being late every day.

Here again is an instance where POSS-*ing* VGerPs pattern more like noun phrases while ACC-*ing* VGerPs pattern like Ss. However, it is hard to see how this difference can be attributed to a difference in the semantics of the two types of gerund phrases. Instead, what this evidence shows is that at some purely syntactic level POSS-*ing* VGerPs have something in common with NPs while ACC-*ing* VGerPs have something in common with Ss.

2.1.3.5   Ellipsis

One way that ACC-*ing* and POSS-*ing* gerunds are similar is that neither allows ellipsis (Abney 1987, 245):

(52)   a. *Pat's fixing the sink was surprising, and Chris's __ was more so.
       b. *Pat fixing the sink was surprising, and Chris __ was more so.

In this way, both kinds of verbal gerunds differ from both NPs and Ss, which do allow N′ and VP ellipsis, respectively:

(53)   a. Pat's repair was surprising, and Chris's __ was more so.
       b. That Pat fixed the the sink was surprising, and that Chris did __ was more so.

This point has been somewhat controversial. Kaiser (1999) claims (contra Abney) that VP ellipsis is in fact possible in ACC-*ing* gerunds. She offers the following contrast:

(54)   a. I was amazed at Pat being so eager and (at) Chris __ too.
       b. *I was amazed at Pat's being so eager and (at) Chris's __ too.

However, judgements differ on these examples. Furthermore, even if (54a) is acceptable, it is most likely not genuine VP ellipsis. It can only be interpreted as as an example of stripping (Hankamer and Sag 1976, Hankamer 1979), a more general form of coordination reduction in which all but one constituent of the second conjunct is deleted. Unlike VP ellipsis, stripping does not require the deleted material to be a VP:

(55)   Pat sent a letter to Sandy, and a package too.

Also unlike VP ellipsis, stripping only applies across coordinate structures (McCawley 1988, 210):

(56)   a. That Pat was singing songs suggests that Chris was too.
       b. *That Pat was singing songs suggests that Chris too.

In both these respects, examples like (54a) behave like stripping and not like VP ellipsis:

(57)   a. I was surprised at Pat sending a letter to Sandy, and a package too.
       b. *Pat singing songs suggests Chris too.

So, if VGerPs do not allow ellipsis, what implication does this fact have for the structure of VGerPs? One conclusion to draw from this is that no verbal gerunds contain an N'. It is not safe to conclude, however, that no verbal gerunds contain a VP. VP ellipsis is restricted to occur only after auxiliary verbs (Sag 1976, Gazdar et al. 1982), and verbal gerund phrases like those in (52) lack an auxiliary verb. Naturally then VP ellipsis is ruled out. And, examples like the following are marginally acceptable:

(58)   ?I am shocked at your having done this, and even more so at LEE's having __.

These examples are not impeccable, but whatever awkwardness they suffer from may be attributed to a general problem with unstressed nonfinite auxiliaries (Zwicky and Levin 1980, Pullum 1991).

2.1.3.6   Summary

To summarize the outcome of this section, both ACC-*ing* and POSS-*ing* verbal gerunds show many properties in common. Therefore, any approach which is unable to give them a uniform analysis will be missing important generalizations. However, ACC-*ing* and POSS-*ing* gerunds do differ in important ways, so an adequate treatment of verbal gerunds must be able to account for those differences. Quantifier scope and pied piping facts show that ACC-*ing* gerund phrases are in some ways like clauses, while POSS-*ing* gerund phrases are more like noun phrases. However, other differences between the two types that have been discussed in the literature, such as in coordination, extraction, and ellipsis behavior, seem to be irrelevant to determining the structure of gerund phrases.

2.2 Previous analyses

As we saw in §2.1, verbal gerunds display a mix of nominal and verbal properties that seems puzzling given many assumptions about syntactic structure. In this section I will review the various approaches that have been proposed to get around these problems.

2.2.1 Methodological principles

An ideal analysis of verbal gerunds in English would be able to account for their mixed verbal/nominal properties, summarized in (59), without the addition of otherwise unmotivated mechanisms.

(59)

VERBS	VERBAL GERUNDS	NOUNS
govern NPs	govern NPs	don't govern NPs
adverbs	adverbs	adjectives
not	*not*	**not*
subjects	subjects/specifiers	specifiers
S distribution	NP distribution	NP distribution

Pullum (1991, 775ff) makes a specific proposal as to what analytic devices ought to be avoided, setting out three 'theoretical desiderata' that any analysis of verbal gerunds should satisfy: strong lexicalism, endocentricity, and null licensing.

Strong lexicalism is the principle that syntactic operations do not have access to the internal structure of words and, conversely, that morphological operations do not apply to syntactic structures. This constraint has its origins in Chomsky (1970) and has received considerable attention in the literature since then (e.g., Jackendoff 1972, Kiparsky 1982, Di Sciullo and Williams 1987, Anderson 1992, Bresnan and Mchombo 1995, Ackerman and Webelhuth 1998).

Endocentricity is the principle that "EVERY constituent has (at least) one distinguished daughter identified as its head." This principle was foreshadowed by the *Tabla Esmeraldina,* an alchemical text attributed to Hermes Trismegistos and known since at least 150 BC, which begins "Quod est inferius est sicut quod est superius," or "as it is below, so it is above." Within the linguistic tradition, the notion of a syntactic head, like lexicalism, has been of particular importance since Chomsky (1970) and has played a central theoretical role in GPSG and especially HPSG. In HPSG, the notion of head can be given a theory internal definition in terms of the Head Feature Principle. In addition, Zwicky (1985) offers several empirical criteria for identifying the head of a construction. First, the syntactic head is generally the morphosyntactic locus, or "the bearer of the marks of syntactic relations," (10) specifically case and agreement markers. Second, the head "is the one constituent that belongs to a category with roughly the same distribution as the construct as a whole" (11). And, finally, in any construction "we should expect the head to be the part that is present in all its occurrences – that is, we should expect the head to be obligatory (and non-heads to be optional)" (13).

By these criteria, the head of an English verbal gerund phrase is the verbal gerund itself. English gerund phrases do not show any relational morphology, so the first criterion is not applicable. But, the gerund is the only obligatory element in a gerund phrase, and I will argue that the gerund has the same category as the phrase it projects.

Null-licensing is a principle intended to restrain the proliferation of phonologically null elements. Pullum proposes that "no phonologically zero constituent should be posited that is neither semantically contentful nor syntactically bound." Specifically, the Principle of Null Licensing as a "methodological guide" that states that:

> ...empty categories should be postulated (if at all) only where at least one of the following three conditions are met:
> 1. The empty category is syntactically bound to another constituent in an unbounded dependency construction (that is, it is an extraction trace).
> 2. The empty category is anaphorically linked to another constituent (that is, it is a null anaphor or controlled *PRO*).
> 3. The empty category is associated with an independently identifiable semantic content (for example, by a construction specific semantic rule, as in [$_{NP}$ *the rich* [$_{N}$ *e*]], semantically interpreted as 'the rich people').

In particular, this principle would rule out phonologically null heads. A stronger position to take would be to rule out all empty categories in general. Sag and Fodor (1994) and Sag (1996) argue that accounts of extraction phenomena that rely on phonologically null traces suffer from inherent problems that are completely avoided by a traceless analysis. So called 'null' anaphora and ellipsis can also be given a coherent account that requires positing no empty categories. However, it is still unclear whether null pronominals can be completely eliminated (see, e.g., Bresnan 1998). So, while I will make no reference to empty categories in the analysis present here, I do not want to place too strong a restriction on their use in general.

Each of these principles has been proposed as a formal universal, in Chomsky's (1965) sense, that constrains the class of possible grammars. While none of them has gone unchallenged, no construction has yet been found that decisively shows any of these principles to be too restrictive. As such they provide a way of evaluating analyses. All things being equal, any analysis that meets these principles is preferable to one that does not. In the next sections, I will show that each of the existing approaches to English verbal gerunds violates one or more of these principles.

2.2.2 No head

The earliest generative analyses of English verbal gerunds took a 'brute force' approach and treated them as exocentric constructions. To take one example,[4] Jackendoff (1977) observed that it is difficult to fit gerunds into a standard X-bar theoretic phrase structure. So, he proposed the exceptional rule schema in (60a) for nominalizations, which (60b) is an instantiation of for POSS-*ing* gerunds:

(60) a. $X^i \rightarrow \text{Aff } V^i$
      b. $N'' \rightarrow \text{-}ing \text{ } V''$

A POSS-*ing* gerund like *Pat's watching television* would have the D-structure in (61).

---

[4]Many similar 'headless' analysis of gerunds have been proposed in the literature (e.g., Lees 1960, Rosenbaum 1967, Chomsky 1970, Horn 1975, Williams 1975, Schachter 1976, Emonds 1976, Akmajian 1977, Jackendoff 1977, Marantz 1978, XTAG Research Group 1995).

(61)

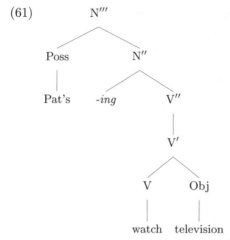

The affix *-ing* then lowers onto the verb via some variation of Affix Hopping.

This analysis clearly violates both lexical integrity and endocentricity. It crucially depends on *-ing* having a position in the syntax that is independent of that of the verb. Also, the N″ in (61) has no head, even though the English verbal gerund does not behave like an exocentric construction.

2.2.3 *Ing* as head

2.2.3.1 Baker (1985)

Baker (1985) proposes an analysis of gerunds that avoids one of the problems of §2.2.2 and assimilates verbal gerunds to conventional X-bar theory. He does this by taking advantage of a loophole in Chomsky's (1981) Projection Principle which was first noted by Pesetsky (1981): "the Projection Principle is consistent with a subcategorized element changing its categorial status in the course of a syntactic derivation" (Baker 1985, 2).

Given this exception, Baker can treat *-ing* as a verbal affix of category N generated under Infl at D-structure. As a verbal affix, *-ing* must move to combine with a verb at S-structure, along the lines of the morphological theory developed by Baker (1988). A verbal gerund like *John's singing the aria* then would have the following derivation:

(62) a. D-structure:

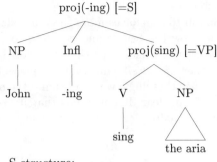

b. S-structure:

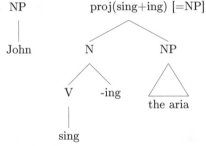

The affix *-ing* lowers to combine with the V *sing*, converting it to an N. Since the categories of the projections of *sing* are simply the category of their head, the conversion of the head from V to N is enough to convert its projections from VP and S to NP and NP. So, by assigning the verbal properties of verbal gerunds to D-structure and their nominal properties to S-structure, Baker can give gerunds an analysis consistent with X-bar theory.

This analysis embodies two very attractive insights: in general, words may have one category at the surface and a different category at a more abstract level, and in particular English verbal gerunds are nounlike on the surface but verblike at heart. Unfortunately, Baker's analysis suffers from several intractable technical flaws. Since these problems are covered in detail by Abney (1987) and Pullum (1991), I will only consider them briefly here.

First, since sentences and noun phrases do not have the same distribution, there must be some head feature which distinguishes I from N. Under Baker's analysis, however, the affix *-ing* is called on to be an I at D-structure and N at S-structure. Not only is the category of the head in (62) changing, the affix *-ing* must also be changing its category in a way left completely mysterious.

Second, the derivation in (62) involves more than just affixation and category conversion: somehow the I node and its non-maximal projections disappear at S-structure. Baker says that "categories that were formerly projections of either -*ing* or *sing* must now be projections of the combined form, *singing,* since this single word subsumes them both" (3). Exactly what this means is unclear, but it seems that it predicts that the derivation in (62) will actually yield the structure in (63).

(63)

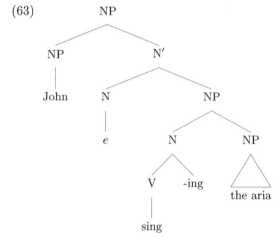

The empty N in (63) corresponds to the Infl node in (62a). The consequences of this double NP structure for government, binding, case marking, subjacency, and other linguistic modules are left unexplored.

Third, under Baker's analysis case assignment must occur at D-structure, to allow a verb to assign accusative case to its object before it is nominalized. However, the subject of the gerund is genitive, and once nominalized a gerund must itself receive case. This suggests that on the contrary case assignment must occur at S-structure. Baker offers no solution to this paradox.

Baker's approach (and the variation proposed by Milsark 1988) does not satisfy our methodological requirements, as it founders on implementation details and depends crucially on syntactic word formation. However, its key underlying insight, that gerunds are verbs only at an abstract level of representation, still seems fundamentally right and indeed will be reflected in the analysis we will eventually adopt in §3.4.

2.2.3.2   Abney (1987)

Building on Baker's (1985) theory of syntactic affixation, Abney (1987) proposes an analysis of English gerunds based on affixation of the ab-

(64)

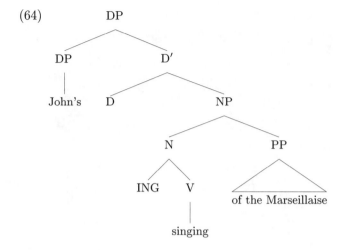

stract nominalizing morpheme *ING* to the *-ing* form of a verb. Abney assumes that categories are marked for three features: ±N, which distinguishes nouns from verbs; a feature ±F which distinguishes lexical from functional categories; and a multi-valued feature for bar level. Abney also proposes a slight modification to the conventional assumptions of X-bar theory to allow certain affixes to combine morphologically with a maximal projection as well as a lexical category.

Abney claims that the properties of English gerunds follow from the assumption that *ING* bears the feature specification [+N] but is unmarked for F and bar level. When *ING* combines with a lexical verb, as in (64), it inherits the verb's values for F and bar level, producing an N^0. Thus, nominal gerunds have all the syntactic properties of underived common nouns. When *ING* affixes to a higher verbal projection, the result is a verbal gerund. The structures of POSS-*ing* and ACC-*ing* gerunds are given in (65). Abney correlates the degree of nominalization with the 'scope' of the nominal affix *ING*: the higher the attachment of *ING*, the more verbal properties the phrase will have. In (65a), *ING* combines with the VP *singing the Marseillaise*. VP is a non-functional maximal projection, VP plus *ING* is a non-functional maximal nominal projection, also known as an NP. Since the subject is ouside the nominalized part of the VGerP, it takes genitive case. In (65b), *ING* combines with the entire IP *John singing the Marseillaise*. IP is a functional maximal projection, so IP plus *ING* is a functional maximal nominal projection, or a DP.

Given his assumptions, Abney's analysis has several fairly minor empirical problems. First, since ACC-*ing* gerunds have an I node, they

(65) a.

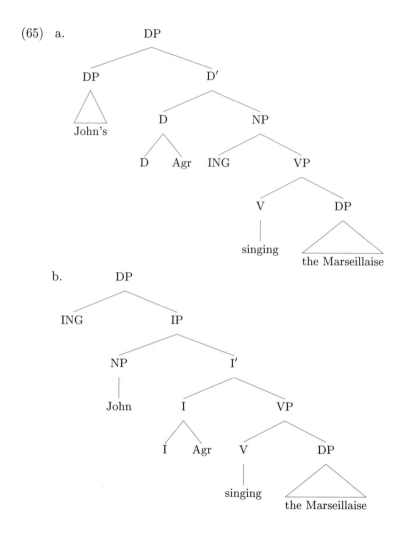

should be able to occur with a lexical finite I (i.e., a modal) or with the non-finite I *to*. However, ACC-*ing* gerunds never can:

(66)   a. *Pat is worried about Chris might being arrested.
       b. *Kim could speaking Italian impressed Sandy.
       c. *Robin approved of Lee to driving a tractor trailor.

To rule out these cases, Abney will have to add a stipulation that nominalized phrases can never include an overt I.

Slightly more vexing problems for Abney arise from the absence of I in POSS-*ing* gerunds. By standard assumptions, the English auxiliary system is closely connected to I. For example, Baker (1988) and Larson (1988) assume that the auxiliary *be* is generated in I. If this is true, then Abney predicts that ACC-*ing* gerunds should allow *be* while POSS-*ing* gerunds should not. However, the two kinds of gerunds show exactly the same behavior with respect to auxiliary verbs:

(67)   a. Lee couldn't ignore Sandy('s) being stoned all the time.
       b. The senator('s) having been on GE's board of directors made conflict of interest charges inevitable.

The same kind of problem comes up with passives: Baker (1988) and Baker et al. (1989) argue that the passive affix -*en* is generated in I. Again, this makes a prediction about a difference between ACC-*ing* and POSS-*ing* gerunds that is not borne out:

(68)   Chris reported Kim('s) being spotted on a flight to Amsterdam.

Of course, Baker's claims about the position of *be* and -*en* have not been universally accepted. The point here is simply to note that Abney's analysis is inconsistent with these proposals.

Even if we do not assume Baker's approach to -*en*, passive POSS-*ing* gerunds still pose a problem for Abney. An example of a passive POSS-*ing* gerund is given in (69a), which presumably has the S-structure in (69b). The subject NP *Sandy's* is generated as the complement of *promoted* and raises to get genitive case from the (phonologically null) nominal Agr adjoined to the (phonologically null) determiner. In a normal possessive phrase, such as *Kim's job*, the null determiner assigns a possessive θ-role to the possessor. However, this assignment is optional (Abney 1987, 93), and the possessor in (69) receives a single θ-role as the object of *promoted*.

In order for (69b) to be a well-formed structure, the Empty Category Principle requires that *Sandy's* must properly govern its trace. This is where a potential problem for Abney's analysis arises. Following Chomsky (1986), antecedent government is blocked by an intervening barrier, where a barrier is a maximal projection immediately dominating a block-

(69) a. Chris talked about Sandy's being promoted.

b.

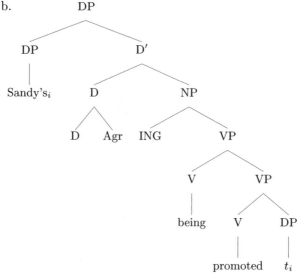

ing category. In (69), the highest VP node is a blocking category, so the highest NP node should be a barrier and (69) ought to be a ruled out as a violation of the ECP.

Abney has two ways to avoid this problem. He could either argue that the VP is not a blocking category, or that the NP is not a maximal projection. In the first case, the VP would have to be assigned a θ-role by some lexical head, presumably *ING*. *ING* is underspecified for the feature F, and so could reasonably be included by a broad enough definition of the notion 'lexical head'. However, it is difficult to see what kind of θ-role it could assign to its VP complement. The second approach would seem to be a more promising tack. Since *ING* combines with the VP by morphological affixation and does not project any syntactic structure of its own, it may be possible to change the definition of 'maximal projection' so as to exclude the highest NP in (69).

Finally, as Kaiser (1999) observes, Abney also has no easy way to rule out nominal modifiers in POSS-*ing* gerunds. As we have seen, N′ modifiers such as attributive adjectives and restrictive relative clauses do not appear in English verbal gerunds. Even though the proposed structure in (65a) includes an NP and not an N′, Abney (1987, 59) notes "NP under the DP-analysis corresponds to N-bar in the standard analysis." So, we would expect to find adjectives modifying NPs, as in (70). Abney has no way to rule out these structures without further

(70)

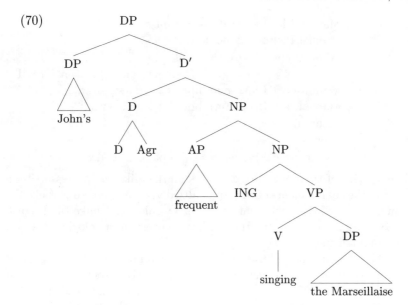

stipulations.

Evaluating Abney's analysis with respect to the principles in §2.2.1 is somewhat challenging: it is unclear whether Abney's analysis satisfies endocentricity, as it is hard to say what is the head of the NP in (65a) or the IP in (65b). However, Yoon (1996) Abney's analysis which clearly satisfies endocentricity. Abney's reliance on null phrasal affixes and null D heads clearly violates null licensing, but does not violate lexical integrity in the same way that Baker (1985) does. There is no claim that the syntax has access to the internal structure of a word. Instead, Abney is claiming that the abstract nominalizing affix *ING* is able to combine with an entire phrase. In this sense, there is nothing radical about Abney's analysis; the view that special clitics are phrasal affixes is both widely held and consistent with even the strongest versions of the lexicalist hypothesis (see, e.g., Anderson 1992).

However, if English has a null nominalizing clitic, one would expect to find a language with richer morphology that has an overt nominalizing clitic. As far as I know, no such language exists. Many languages have overt nominalizing affixes, but in every case this morphology can be shown to be lexical and not phrasal.

One such language is Quechua. Quechua has a number of nominalization constructions, one of which, exemplified in (71), is comparable to the English POSS-*ing* gerund.

(71) a. Manuil Pidru-man libru-ta   qu-n
          Manuel Pedro-DAT book-ACC give-3
          'Manuel gives Pedro the book.'
                                    (Lefebvre and Muysken 1988, 16)
      b. Manuil-pa   Pidru-man libru-ta   qu-sqa-n-ta
          Manuel-GEN Pedro-DAT book-ACC give-NMLZ-3-ACC
          yacha-ni
          know-1
          'I know that Manuel gives the book to Pedro.'

The subject of the nominalized verb is marked like the possessor in an
NP and the complements of the nominalized verb are marked just like the
complements of the equivalent finite verb would be. Unlike the English
POSS-*ing* gerund, this construction has an overt morphological marker,
the nominalizing affix -*sqa*-.

This nominalizing affix -*sqa*- is a good candidate for being an overt
analog to the covert English nominalizer *ING*. However, Lefebvre and
Muysken (1988, 82ff) give numerous arguments that -*sqa*- and the other
Quechua nominalizers must be treated as lexical affixes and not as
phrasal clitics. For one, if -*sqa*- is a clitic then the agreement and case
markers that follow it must also be clitics (Zwicky and Pullum 1983).
But, Lefebvre and Muysken show that in contrast to the genitive clitic
-*qpa*, the accusative marker -*ta* must be an affix.

This is not to say that no languages have nominalizing clitics. For
example, take the Classical Tibetan nominalizer -*pa*:

(72) a. saŋsrgyas-kyis tšhos   bšad
          buddha-ERG   dharma.ABS tell
          'The Buddha taught the dharma.'   (Beyer 1992, 300)
      b. [saŋsrgyas-kyis tšhos   bšad-pa]-kyis dgesloŋ
          buddha-ERG   dharma.ABS tell-NOM-ERG monk.ABS
          myaŋan-las   ndas
          suffering-ABL pass
          'The monk entered nirvana because of the teaching of the
          dharma by the Buddha.'   (Beyer 1992, 303)

-*Pa* shows none of the properties of an affix and is clearly a phrasal
clitic. For example, it can be used to nominalize a coordinate clause:

(73) a. ltaba yaŋs-šiŋ   spyodlam žib-pa-r   mdzod
          view vast-CONJ conduct   precise-NOM-ADV cause
          'Make your view broad and your practice precise.'
                                    (Beyer 1992, 344)

b. ndre   ša-la   za-žsiŋ   khra-la   nthuŋ-ba
   demon flesh-LOC eat-CONJ colored-LOC drink-NOM
   'demons who feed on flesh and gorge on blood'

(Beyer 1992, 334)

And in Tibetan, unlike in Quechua, case markers are also clearly phrasal clitics. For example, a coordinate noun phrase only takes a case marker on the last noun:

(74) tšos   ri-daŋ   luŋpa-la   dar
      dharma mountain-CONJ valley-LOC spread
      'The dharma spread to mountain and valley.'

(Beyer 1992, 240)

However, internally Tibetan nominalized clauses show no nominal properties. The nominalizing clitics, including -pa, attach to a tensed verb and fill a morphological slot that is shared only by sentence-level illocutionary force markers and coordinating conjunctions. And, the same nominalizer -pa is used to form complement clauses and relative clauses:

(75) a. [saŋsrgyas-kyis tšhos   bšad-pa]-r   grags
          buddha-ERG   dharma.ABS tell-NOM-ADV be.known
          'It is well known that the Buddha taught the dharma.'

(Beyer 1992, 334)

      b. dgesloŋ-gis [tšhos$_i$ [saŋsrgyas-kyis t_i bšad-pa]]   bstod
          monk-ERG   dharma Buddha-ERG   tell-NOM.ABS praise
          'The monk praised the dharma which the Buddha taught.'

(Beyer 1992, 315)

So, -pa is probably best seen as a prosodically bound complementizer comparable to English *that* rather than as a true nominalizing clitic deriving a mixed category, like *ING*.

The conclusion to draw from this brief cross-linguistic excursion is this: from my admittedly limited survey of nominalization types, it appears that no language has an overt nominalizing clitic corresponding to Abney's English *ING*.[5] Since English is rife with zero conversion in general, it would not be surprising to find that it also has a null nominalizing clitic. It would be surprising, however, to find that this nominalizer is always phonologically null, even in languages with lots of category changing morphology.

---

[5]Kaiser (1997, 1999) argues that Korean -*um* is a nominalizing clitic. However, the facts she presents are consistent with its being either an affix or a clitic. In addition, there are general problems in distinguishing affixes from clitics in Korean (see Kim 1995b, 1995c).

2.2.4 Gerund as head

2.2.4.1 Pullum (1991)

Pullum (1991) proposes an analysis of verbal gerunds that exploits the flexibility of the GPSG Head Feature Convention (HFC) to allow V to project NP under certain circumstances. Pullum starts with the following rule for ordinary possessed NPs:

(76) N[BAR:2] → N[BAR:2, POSS:+], H[BAR:1]

The head of the phrase is only specified for the feature BAR. The HFC is a default condition that requires that the mother and the head daughter match on all features, so long as they do not conflict with any "absolute condition on feature specifications" (780). So, for instance, for the rule in (76) this will ensure that the head daughter will match the mother in its major category and that the phrase will be headed by an N. Given this background, Pullum observes that POSS-*ing* VGerPs can be accounted for by introducing a slightly modified version of the previous rule:

(77) N[BAR:2] → (N[BAR:2, POSS:+],) H[VFORM:prp]

This rule differs from the rule in (76) only in the feature specification on the head daughter: in (77), the head daughter is required to be [VFORM:prp]. An independently motivated Feature Co-occurrence Restriction (FCR) given in (78) requires that any phrase with a VFORM value must be verbal.

(78) [VFORM] ⊃ [V:+, N:−]

This constraint overrides the HFC, so the rule in (77) will only admit phrases with -*ing* form verb heads. However, the left-hand side of the rule is the same as the left-hand side in (76), so (77) will give verbal gerunds the following structure:

(79)

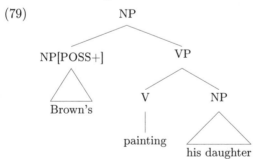

This reflects the traditional description of VGerPs as 'verbal inside, nominal outside' quite literally by giving VGerPs a VP node dominated by an NP node. However, Pullum's analysis only applies to POSS-*ing* VGerPs and has nothing to say about ACC-*ing* VGerPs at all. He suggests that ACC-*ing* and POSS-*ing* VGerPs "must be analyzed quite differently" (766), but by treating them as unrelated constructions, he fails to capture their similarities.

This is not merely a shortcoming of the presentation. There does not seem to be any natural way to assimilate ACC-*ing* VGerPs to Pullum's analysis. The simplest way to extend (77) to cover ACC-*ing* VGerPs is to add the following rule:

(80)   N[BAR:2] → (N[BAR:2]), H[VFORM:prp]

Since the default case for NPs is accusative, this rule will combine an accusative NP with an -*ing* form VP. This rule neatly accounts for the similarities between the two type of verbal gerunds, but not the differences.

Following the direction of Hale and Platero's (1986) proposal for Navajo nominalized clauses, we might try (81) instead.

(81)   N[BAR:2] → H[SUBJ:+, VFORM:prp]

The feature SUBJ indicates whether a phrase contains a subject and is used to distinguish VPs from Ss. A VP is V[BAR:2, SUBJ:−] while an S is V[BAR:2, SUBJ:+]. So, (81) would assign an ACC-*ing* VGerP the structure in (82).

(82)

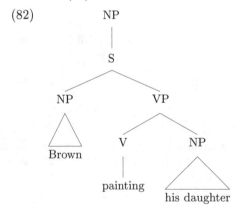

It is plausible that this rule might account for the differences in semantic type and quantifier scope potential between the two types of gerund phrases. It less clear though how it can account for the difference in pied piping, since nothing in the GPSG treatment of relative clauses rules out examples like (42b), repeated here (see Pollard and Sag 1994, 214ff):

(83)   *The person (for) who(m) to be late every day Pat didn't like

got promoted anyway.

Pullum's analysis cannot, however, properly account for PRO-*ing* VGerPs. Since the possessive NP in (77) is optional, it treats PRO-*ing* VGerPs as a subtype of POSS-*ing* VGerPs even though, as we have seen, PRO-*ing* VGerPs have more in common with ACC-*ing* VGerPs. Furthermore, this analysis provides no account for the control properties of PRO-*ing* VGerPs. Some subjectless gerund complements, like some subjectless infinitive complements, must be interpreted as if their missing subject were coreferential with an argument of the higher verb:

(84)   Chris tried $\left\{ \begin{array}{c} \text{to find} \\ \text{finding} \end{array} \right\}$ a Nautilus machine in Paris without success.

In both sentences in (84) the subject of *find* must be coindexed with the subject of *tried,* namely *Chris* (for more discussion, see §2.3.3). In HPSG control for infinitive complements is determined by the Control Agreement Principle, which ensures that the AGR value of *to* in (85) is identified with the AGR value of *try* (Gazdar et al. 1985, 121).

(85)

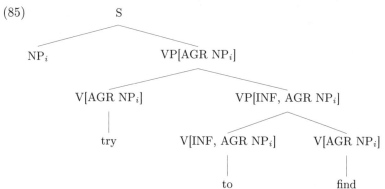

Other constraints identify the AGR value of *try* with its subject and the AGR value of *to* with the unexpressed subject of *find.* While this works for infinitive complements, it cannot be extended to account for control in gerunds. The agreement FCR in (86) will block projection of the gerund's AGR value to the top-level NP node.

(86)   [AGR] ⊃ [V:+, N:−]

Because complement control is mediated by AGR specifications, there will be no way to capture the parallel behavior of subjectless infinitives and gerunds.

Finally, structures like (82) raise doubt as to whether the notion of head embodied by the HFC has any content at all. In this case, the only head specification shared by the mother and the head daughter is [BAR:2], and this match comes about not by the HFC but by the accidental cooperation of the rule in (81) with the FCR in (87).

(87) [+SUBJ] ⊃ [V:+, N:−, BAR:2]

I think it is fair to classify (81) as an exocentric rule. So, the only clear way to extend Pullum's analysis to account for ACC-*ing* VGerPs violates one of the theoretical desiderata that are the primary motivators for his analysis in the first place.[6]

2.2.4.2 Lapointe (1993)

Lapointe (1993) observes three problems with Pullum's analysis. The first problem is that, as discussed above, it vitiates the principle of phrasal endocentricity. Lapointe's second objection is that Pullum's proposal is much too general. It has no way of representing the fact that some types of mixed category constructions are much more common than others. Nothing in it prohibits outlandish and presumably non-attested rules such as:

(88) a. VP → H[NFORM:plur], PP
      b. N′ → (QP), H⁰[VFORM:psp]

And, nothing in it explains why constructions parallel to the English POSS-*ing* verbal gerund are found in language after language (we will look at the range of cross-linguistic variation in more detail in §3.1).

To avoid these shortcomings of Pullum's analysis, Lapointe proposes a more conservative modification to the standard notion of endocentricity. He proposes introducing dual lexical categories like ⟨N|V⟩, a V which projects a VP dominated by an NP. Specifically, Lapointe offers the following definition:

(89) A **dual lexical category** is an object of the form $\langle X|Y\rangle^0$, where

   a. X, Y are major lexical categories,
   b. X determines the external syntactic properties of the phrase of which the item is the lexical head, and
   c. Y determines the internal syntactic properties of that phrase.

This approach avoids some of the problems associated with default projection by restricting the conditions under which categorial 'change-over' can occur.

---

[6]In addition, there are quite general formal problems with the default nature of the GPSG Head Feature Convention (Shieber 1986, Bouma 1993).

(90)   DLC Feature Introduction Conditions (DLC-FIC)
Let X, Y be distinct major lexical categories, F a feature, and
γ a set of features.

    a. The only type of ID rule that can introduce [DLC] has the
form:

$$[\langle X|X\rangle; \mathsf{BAR:2}] \to \ldots, \mathsf{H}[\langle X|Y\rangle; \mathsf{BAR:2}], \ldots$$

    b. No ID rule can have the form

$$\langle X|X\rangle \to \ldots, \mathsf{H}[F, \gamma], \ldots$$

where F implies $\langle X|Y\rangle$, unless γ includes $\langle X|Y\rangle$.

However, Lapointe restricts himself to discussion of genitive subject
VGerPs. As a consequence, his analysis suffers from the same problems
as Pullum's. In addition, since Lapointe's necessarily brief presentation
leaves some formal details unspecified, it is not at all clear that a rule
like (81) would even be permissible under his system.

2.2.4.3   Wescoat (1994)

Wescoat (1994) points out a problem with Pullum's analysis that also
applies to Lapointe's analysis: in excluding articles and adjectives from
gerunds, they "make no allowance for a variant grammar of English that
admits archaic forms like [(91)], attested between the 15th and early
20th centuries" (588).

(91)   a. the untrewe forgyng and contryvyng certayne testamentys
        and last wyll [15th cent.]
      b. my wicked leaving my father's house [17th cent.]
      c. the being weighted down by the stale and dismal oppression
        of the rememberance [19th cent.]

Wescoat goes on to note that "such structures coexisted with all modern
gerund forms, so it is only plausible that the current and former grammars of gerunds should be largely compatible, in a way that Pullum's
approach cannot model."[7]

Wescoat proposes to preserve phrasal endocentricity by modifying
Kornai and Pullum's (1990) axiomatization of X-bar syntax to allow
a single word to project two different unordered lexical categories and
therefore two different maximal phrases. He proposes that verbal gerunds
have a structure like (92a), parallel to the clause in (92b).

---

[7]For more on archaic gerunds, see §2.4.

(92) a.

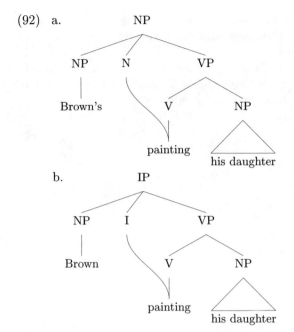

b.

In these trees, the N and I nodes, respectively, are extrasequential. That is to say, they are unordered with respect to their sisters. This structure preserves syntactic projection, but at the cost of greatly complicating the geometry of the required phrase structure representations in ways that do not seem to be independently motivated.[8]

Even assuming Wescoat's formal mechanism can be justified, the analysis shown in (92a) runs into problems with POSS-*ing* VGerPs. In order to account for the non-occurrence of adjectives and determiners with gerunds in Late Modern English, Wescoat adds a stipulation that the N node associated with a gerund must be extrasequential. Since adjectives and determiners must precede the N they attach to, this stipulation prevents them from occurring with gerunds. But, possessors also have to precede the head noun in their NP, so this stipulation should also prevent gerunds from occurring with possessors. Since there is no way an ordering restriction could distinguish between adjectives and determiners on the one hand and possessors on the other, Wescoat has no choice but to treat possessors in POSS-*ing* VGerPs as subjects with unusual case marking, not as specifiers. In so doing, he fails to predict that POSS-*ing* VGerPs, unlike ACC-*ing* VGerPs, share many properties

---

[8]But see Wescoat (1996) for an application of lexical sharing to Hindi noun incorporation.

of head-specifier constructions. For example, POSS-*ing* gerunds are subject to the same pied piping constraints as NPs, while ACC-*ing* gerunds behave more like clauses.

On the other hand, Wescoat's approach would extend to cover the ACC-*ing* VGerPs that are problematic for other analyses. A natural variant of (82) using lexical sharing would be:

(93)

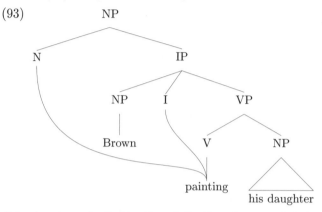

In this structure, both the N and the I nodes associated with *painting* are extrasequential. This tree seems to be fully consistent with all of Wescoat's phrase structure tree axioms. But, because it is not clear from his discussion how non-categorial features get projected, it is hard to say whether this kind of analysis could account for the differences between the two types of VGerPs. For instance, the contrast in (42), repeated in (94), is typically attributed to the fact that projection of *WH* features is clause-bounded.

(94) a. The person whose chronic lateness Pat didn't like got promoted anyway.
   b. *The person (for) who(m) to be late every day Pat didn't like got promoted anyway.

This is what motivates the introduction of an S node in (82). However, it is not obvious that the introduction of an IP in (93) will prevent any features from projecting from the head *painting* directly to the top-most NP. If the N, I, and V nodes in (93) are really sharing the same lexical token, then the same head features should be projected to the NP, IP, and VP nodes. Otherwise, in what sense are the three leaf nodes 'sharing' the same lexical token? Without further development of these issues, it is hard to evaluate Wescoat's analysis.

Finally, Wescoat's approach runs into a fatal problem when faced with coordinate gerund phrases.[9] Take an example like (95).

(95)   Pat's never watching movies or reading books

Since the adverb *never* is modifying the whole coordinated VP, the only plausible structure Wescoat could assign to this sentence is (96).

(96)

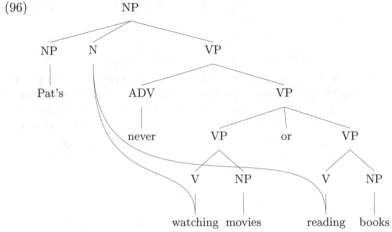

But, this structure is clearly ruled out by Wescoat's constraints: the mapping from leaf nodes to lexical tokens need not be one-to-one, but it must still be a function. That is, while a lexical token may be linked to more than one leaf node, each leaf node must be linked to one and only one lexical token. Therefore Wescoat's approach cannot account for examples like (95), and there is no obvious way that it could be extended to handle this kind of construction.[10]

2.2.4.4   Summary

As we saw in section 2.1, verbal gerunds display a mix of nominal and verbal properties that seems puzzling given many assumptions about syntactic structure. We have seen various approaches have been proposed to get around these problems. Very similar proposals have been made by Hale and Platero (1986) for Navajo nominalized clauses, by Aoun (1981) for Arabic participles, by van Riemsdijk (1983) for German adjectives, and by Lefebvre and Muysken (1988) for Quechua nominalized clauses.

While these analyses differ greatly in their technical details, they all assign VGerPs some variation of the following structure:

---

[9]This problem was pointed out to me by Wescoat himself.

[10]Bresnan (1997) presents an analysis of mixed categories which is similar to Wescoat's (1994) but does not suffer from this problem in the same way. However, Bresnan's analysis cannot be applied to English verbal gerunds (see Malouf 1998).

(97)

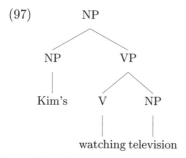

watching television

This reflects the traditional description of VGerPs as 'verbal inside, nominal outside' quite literally by giving VGerPs a VP node dominated by an NP node. However, since (97) is quite unlike the structures one typically finds in English, each of these analyses requires abandoning a fundamentally desirable theoretical assumption or adopting a highly abstract structure for which independent motivation is difficult to find. If we accept X-bar theory in general, then the 'null hypothesis' should be that structures like (97) do not exist. If there were strong evidence that (97) was indeed the structure of an English verbal gerund, then we would have no choice but reject the hypothesis. However, as we saw in §2.1.2, there is no clear evidence that verbal gerunds include a VP. Therefore, an analysis which can account for the properties of verbal gerunds without violating the principles of X-bar theory is preferable a priori to one that posits a structure like (97). In the remainder of this chapter I will explore an analysis of verbal gerunds based on an alternative view, one that takes into account the varying sources of syntactic information by exploiting the rich HPSG representations and thus calls into question the assumption underlying analyses involving categorial 'change-over'.

2.3   A mixed category analysis

The theoretical framework described in §1.3 provides a foundation for an analysis of verbal gerunds which does not require any categorial 'change-over'. It does this by factoring syntactic properties into separate categorial, selectional, and constructional information. Words in HPSG select for arguments of a particular category. Therefore, categorial information, projected from the lexical head following the conventions of standard X-bar theory, determines the external distribution of a phrase. Selectional information, from a lexical head's valence features, determines what kinds of other phrases can occur in construction with that head. Morphological properties determine what kinds of inflection and derivation a lexeme is eligible to undergo. Finally, constructional information, represented as constraints on particular constructions, controls the combination of syntactic units.[11] Within each of these three domains, VGerPs show fairly consistent behavior. What is unusual about verbal gerunds is their combination of noun-like categorial properties with verb-like selectional properties. In this section, I will show how this division of syntactic labor can be exploited to provide a lexical account of the mixed nature of verbal gerunds without the need for exotic structure.

Within HPSG, the categorial (i.e., distributional) properties of verbal gerunds are determined by their lexically specified HEAD value. Like all other linguistic objects, types of HEAD values can be arranged into a multiple inheritance type hierarchy expressing the generalizations across categories. The distribution of VGerPs then can be accounted for by the (partial) hierarchy of HEAD values in (98).[12]

(98)

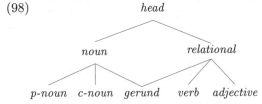

Since *gerund* is a subtype of *noun* along with *p-noun* (proper noun) and *c-noun* (common noun), a phrase projected by a gerund will be able to occur anywhere an NP is selected for. Thus, VGerPs will have the external distribution of NPs. Adverbs potentially modify objects of category *relational,* which include verbs, adjectives, and verbal gerunds, among other things. Since adjectives in their role as modifiers only modify *c-nouns,* VGerPs will contain adverbial rather than adjectival modifiers. Since *verb* is a distinct subclass of *relational* disjoint from *gerund,* VGerPs will not have the distribution of true VPs. This cross-classification directly reflects the traditional view of gerunds as intermediate between nouns and verbs. In this respect, it is nothing new: in the second century BC Dionysius Thrax analyzed the Greek participle as a "separate part of speech which '...partakes of the nature of verbs and

---

[11] This factorization of information is by no means unique to HPSG (cf. the distinction between f-structure and c-structure in Lexical Functional Grammar or between constituency and valency in Pullum and Zwicky 1991).

[12] HPSG inheritance hierarchies, as presented by, e.g., Pollard and Sag (1987), often use a limited form of multiple inheritance. In those hierarchies (and in the one in §3.4.3), types inherit from supertypes in more than one distinct partition. The type *gerund* in (98), in contrast, inherits from more than one supertype in the same partition. This hierarchy could be recast using multiple partitions, but it is not clear that there would be an advantage to doing so.

nouns'" (Michael 1970, 75). However, by formalizing this intuitive view as a cross-classification of HEAD values, we can localize the idiosyncratic behavior of verbal gerunds to the lexicon.

Recall the properties of verbal gerunds that we are trying to account for, repeated here from (21) on page 31:

(99) a. A verbal gerund takes the same complements as the verb from which it is derived.

   b. Verbal gerunds are modified by adverbs and not by adjectives.

   c. The entire verbal gerund phrase has the external distribution of an NP.

   d. The subject of the gerund is optional and, if present, can be either a genitive or an accusative NP.

The position of *gerund* in the hierarchy of HEAD values provides an immediate account of the facts in (21b) and (21c). The remaining two gerund properties in (21) can be accounted for most simply by the lexical rule in (100).

(100)
$$
\begin{bmatrix} \text{HEAD} & \begin{bmatrix} verb \\ \text{VFORM } prp \end{bmatrix} \\ \text{VALENCE} & \begin{bmatrix} \text{SUBJ} & \langle \boxed{1}\text{NP}\rangle \\ \text{COMPS} & \boxed{2} \\ \text{SPR} & \langle\,\rangle \end{bmatrix} \end{bmatrix} \implies \begin{bmatrix} \text{HEAD} & gerund \\ \text{VALENCE} & \begin{bmatrix} \text{SUBJ} & \langle\boxed{1}\rangle \\ \text{COMPS} & \boxed{2} \\ \text{SPR} & \langle\boxed{1}\rangle \end{bmatrix} \end{bmatrix}
$$

This rule produces a lexical entry for a verbal gerund from the *-ing* form of the verb. Any verb with an *-ing* form, including the passive auxiliary *be* and the perfective auxiliary *have*, will also have a verbal gerund. This means that since modals have only finite forms and lack present participles, this rule correctly predicts that modals will not occur in VGerPs. The verbal gerund differs syntactically from the participle in two ways: it is of category *gerund* and it subcategorizes for both a specifier and a subject. Since a verbal gerund selects for the same complements as the verb it is derived from, the phrase formed by a verbal gerund and its complements will look like a VP. And, since a gerund selects for both a subject and a specifier, it will be eligible to head either a *nonfin-head-subj-cx,* which combines a head with an accusative NP subject, or a *noun-poss-cx,* which combines a head with a genitive NP specifier. Since the subject and specifier are identified with each other, no verbal gerund will be able to combine with both a subject and a specifier. POSS-*ing* VGerPs will inherit all the constraints that apply to possessive constructions in general, for example, restrictions on the specifier NP (Zwicky and Pullum 1996) and on pied piping (Sag 1997). The

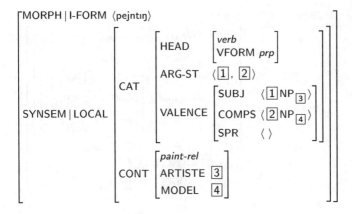

FIGURE 7 Lexical entry for *painting* (participle).

differences in agreement found between verbal gerunds with accusative subjects and genitive specifiers follow from the differences between the two constructions: the *noun-poss-cx* construction licenses a phrase with nominal semantics while the *nonfin-head-subj-cx* construction licenses a phrase with propositional semantics.

2.3.1 Some examples

To see how these constraints interact to account for the syntax of verbal gerunds, it will be useful to consider an example of each type. First, consider the (partial) lexical entry for the present participle of the verb *paint,* in Figure 7. This entry states that there is a word (pronounced /pejntɪŋ/) which is the present participle form of a verb. It selects for two arguments, a subject and a complement, which fill the ARTISTE and MODEL roles of the verb's meaning. Most of the information in a lexical entry like Figure 7 is inherited from higher lexical types.[13] In general, only the phonology, lexical type, and perhaps subcategorization frame need to be stipulated for each lexical entry. From the entry in Figure 7, the lexical rule in (100) produces the matching entry in Figure 8. The entries in Figure 7 and Figure 8 differ only in the shaded features. The output of the lexical rule is of category *gerund,* rather than *verb,* and the gerund selects for both a subject and a specifier. All other information

---

[13]Note that these lexical classes will in general not be isomorphic to traditional lexical categories like V, N, or P. For some of the details of the structure of the lexicon, see e.g. Flickinger (1987), Pollard and Sag (1987), Riehemann (1998), Davis (1996), Wechsler (1995).

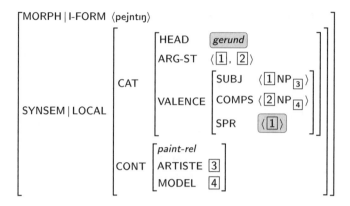

FIGURE 8 Lexical entry for *painting* (gerund).

about the verbs gets carried over from the input to the lexical rule.[14]

Now we turn to the constructions from the inventory discussed in §1.4.2 which the gerund in Figure 8 is eligible to head. There are two cases, POSS-*ing* VGerPs and accusative subject VGerPs. First we will look at the structure of the VGerP *Brown's painting his daughter,* shown in Figure 9. The head of this phrase, *painting,* is a verbal gerund formed by the lexical rule in (100). It combines with its complement NP (marked ③) via the *head-comp-cx* construction. It then combines with a genitive specifier to form a *noun-poss-cx* construction. Note that the formulation of the Valence Principle in §1.4.3 allows *Pat's* to satisfy both the subject and the specifier requirement of the gerund simultaneously. However, since the construction this phrase is an instance of is a sub-type of *head-spr, Brown's* will only have the properties of specifier.

An equivalent example with an accusative subject is given in Figure 10, for the VGerP *Brown painting his daughter.* This example differs from the previous example only in the way the subject combines with the head. The *nonfin-head-subj-cx* construction combines a non-finite head with an accusative case subject. As before, *Brown* cancels both the subject and the specifier requirement of the head, but in this case it will have only subject properties.

As these examples show, the constructions that combine a verbal gerund with its complements and its subject or specifier are the same constructions used for building NPs, VPs, and Ss. This reflects the traditional view that VGerPs are built out of pieces of syntax 'reused'

---

[14]The default nature of the rule in (100) is only for expository clarity. A non-default version of the rule could be written without running into the 'carryover' problems discussed by, for example, Meurers (1994, 33).

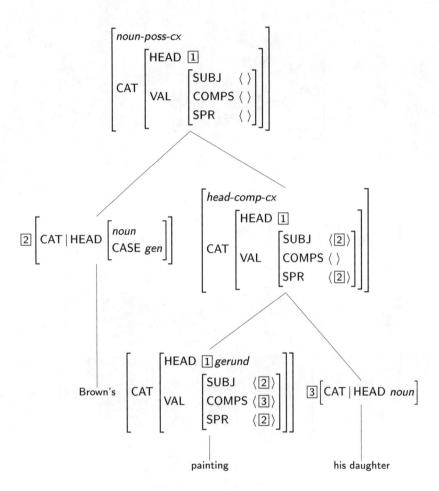

FIGURE 9 *Brown's painting his daughter*

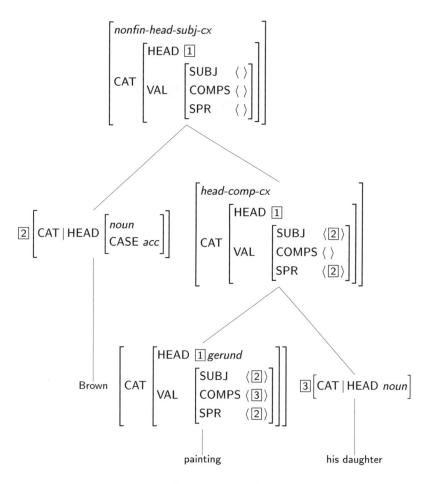

FIGURE 10 *Brown painting his daughter*

from other parts of the grammar.

In one sense, under this analysis a verbal gerund together with its complements really is like V′. Both are instances of the same construction type and both are subject to any constraints associated with that construction. In the same way, a verbal gerund plus an accusative subject really do form an S, while a verbal gerund plus a genitive subject really do form an NP. So, these two types of verbal gerund phrases inherit the constraints on semantic type, pied piping, and quantifier scope associated with the construction type of which they are an instance.

However, in a more important sense, a verbal gerund plus its complements forms a VGer′, which combines with an accusative or genitive subject to form a VGerP:

(101) a.

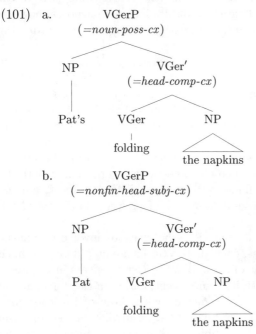

The analysis presented here allows this similarity to be captured without weakening HPSG's strong notion of endocentricity.

2.3.2 Coordination

As we saw in §2.2.4, coordination has proven to be a stumbling block for some previous analyses of English verbal gerunds. In this section I will briefly sketch how, given a few basic assumptions, the analysis of gerunds presented here is able to account for coordinated gerund phrases.

First, suppose we take the strong form of the analysis of coordination outlined by Pollard and Sag (1994, 201ff):

(102) Coordination Principle
In a coordinate structure, the CATEGORY and NONLOCAL value of each conjunct daughter is identical to that of the mother.

This clearly is too strong, as it requires all conjuncts to be exactly of the same category and so, for example, falsely rules out coordination of a VP headed by a main verb with one headed by an auxiliary verb:

(103) a. Francis arrived late today but will be on time tomorrow.
b. Leslie likes that picture and is trying to buy it.

In these examples the first conjunct is [AUX −] while the second is [AUX +]. So, there is no possible value that AUX could have on the coordinate VP that would satisfy (102).[15] For our purposes, however, these details are unimportant; the strong version of the Coordination Principle is good enough.

Given this view of coordination (or something like it), the structure of a sentence with a coordinate VP would look like Figure 11. Recall that the features HEAD, SUBJ, and COMPS are part of the value of CAT. Thus, the Coordination Principle requires the values of all three features to be identical on all conjuncts in a coordinate structure. Each verb combines with its complement in the usual way, and then the SUBJ value of each verb is merged with the SUBJ requirement of the coordinate VP as a whole. The coordinate VP then combines with a subject in exactly the same way as a non-coordinate VP combines with a subject, and the single subject then is an argument of each of the verbs in the coordinate structure.

Since under the present analysis verbal gerunds involve no unusual projection or constructions, coordinate VGerPs are no different from coordinate VPs. An example of a coordinate VGerP appears in Figure 12. Each gerund combines with its complement, and then the SUBJ and SPR values of the two conjuncts are merged with those of the coordinate structure as a whole. The coordinate VGer' *watching movies and reading books* is then eligible to combine with either a subject or specifier in exactly the same way a non-coordinate VGer' like *watching movies* would be. So, the present analysis is able to account for data that was problematic for Wescoat (1994).

---

[15]See, e.g., Sag et al. (1985) or Blevins and Sag (1996) for further discussion of this issue.

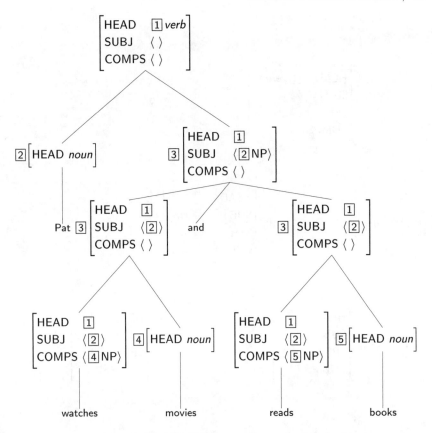

FIGURE 11 *Pat watches movies and reads books*

2.3.3 Gerunds and control

The next example, in Figure 13, is of the subjectless verbal gerund phrase *painting his daughter*. In this case, both the SUBJ and SPR requirements are left unsatisfied. But since the *head-comp-control-cx* construction is a subtype of *clause*, the constraint on clauses in (13) on page 14, repeated here, requires that the subject be a non-canonical *synsem* (either *pro* or *gap*).

(104)   *clause* →

$$\begin{bmatrix} \text{SYNSEM} \mid \text{LOCAL} & \begin{bmatrix} \text{CAT} \mid \text{VALENCE} \mid \text{SUBJ list}(\textit{non-canonical}) \\ \text{CONT } \textit{psoa} \end{bmatrix} \end{bmatrix}$$

The phrase in Figure 13 has an empty SLASH value, so its subject and specifier cannot be a *gap* and must be a *pro*. By definition no lexical or

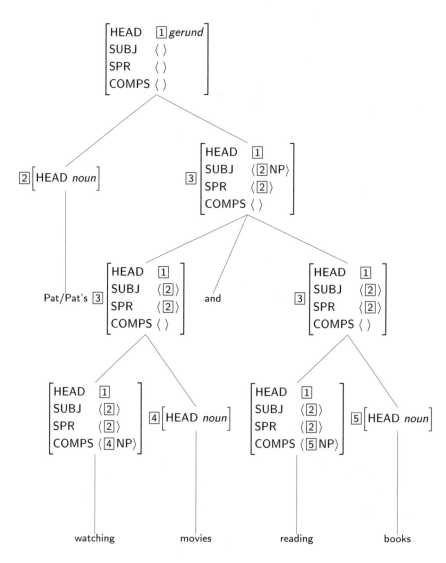

FIGURE 12 *Pat/Pat's watching movies and reading books*

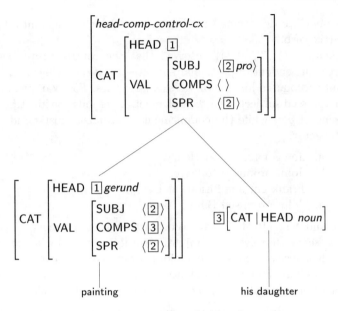

FIGURE 13 *painting his daughter*

phrasal sign has a SYNSEM value which is compatible with a *pro* synsem, so neither requirement can ever be filled by an expression outside the VGerP.

Since the unexpressed subject of the phrase is a *pro*, it will be governed by Sag and Pollard (1991) and Pollard and Sag's (1994) semantic theory of complement control just like the unexpressed subjects of infinitive complements in Equi constructions. Wasow and Roeper (1972) observe the following parallel between PRO-*ing* VGerPs and subjectless infinitives:

(105) a. Lee hates loud singing.
       b. Lee hates singing loudly.
       c. Lee hates to sing loudly.

In both (105b) and (105c), the understood subject of the embedded verb must be *Lee*. In (105a), though, the understood subject of the nominal gerund *singing* can be anyone. In this section I will first sketch the HPSG theory of infinitive complement control and then show how it might be interpreted to cover cases like (105b).

The theory of complement control developed by Pollard and Sag (1994) treats control as basically a semantic phenomenon. They argue that the reference possibilities of the unexpressed subject of an infinitive complement are determined (at least in part) by the semantic type of the matrix verb.

Jackendoff (1972, 1974) observed that the control properties of a verb are independent of particular subcategorization frames and can be uniformly accounted for in terms of thematic roles. For example, in (106) the unexpressed subject of the complement of *got* must be identified with the theme of *got,* while the complement of *promise* must be identified with the actor:

(106)   a.   Joe got furious at Henry.
        b.   John promised to leave.
        c.   Frank got Joe furious at Henry.
        d.   John promised Bill to leave.

Pollard and Sag (1994, 284ff) argue further that a theory of control based on semantic roles can straightforwardly account for a wide range of facts that pose a serious problem for a strictly syntactic approach. For example, Pollard and Sag's semantic control theory is able to account for control in nominal complements as well as verbal complements:

(107)   a.   Sandy's promise to leave the party early caused quite an uproar.
        b.   Sandy's promise to Tracy to leave the party early caused quite an uproar.
        c.   The promise by Sandy to leave the party early caused quite an uproar.
        d.   The promise Sandy made, to leave the party early, caused quite an uproar.
        e.   The promise to leave the party early, which Kim knew would be immediately forthcoming from Sandy, was going to cause quite an uproar.

The control properties of the noun *promise* in (107a) are parallel to those of the verb *promise* in (106b). However, as (107b–e) demonstrate, it is not generally possible to characterize the position of the controller in purely syntactic terms. A semantic theory of control can even account for cases of what Dowty (1989) calls 'remote control':

(108)   A: Sandy promised Tracy something.
        B: What was it?
        A: I think it was to leave the party early.

Here the controller and the infinitival complement are not even part of the same utterance. In each case, though, the controller fills the actor role of *promise.*

The HPSG control theory is summarized in (109) (Pollard and Sag 1994, 288).[16]

(109)   CONTROL THEORY
        If the CONTENT of an unsaturated phrase is an argument of a control relation, then the subject of that phrase is coindexed with the INFLUENCED, COMMITTOR, or EXPERIENCER value, according as the control relation is of sort *influence, commitment,* or *orientation,* respectively.

This constraint was intended to apply to the combination of a subjectless infinitive and verb with the appropriate semantics. For a verb like *got,* whose content is an *influence*-type relation, the unexpressed subject of the VP complement must construed as the person being influenced, as it is in (106c). For a *commit*-type verb like *promise,* the unexpressed subject must be construed as the person being committed, as in (106d).

Since (109) makes no reference to the syntactic category of the unsaturated argument, it should apply to verbal gerunds as well as infinitival phrases. Many of the obligatory control cases discussed by Wasow and Roeper (1972) follow directly from (109). In (105b), *hates* expresses an *orientation* relation, and by (109) the unexpressed subject of its clausal complement must be coindexed with its experiencer role. Some other verbs that fall into this class are:[17]

(110)   *(can't) bear, begrudge, detest, dislike, dread, enjoy, envisage, escape, (not) fancy, forget, hate, like, love, (not) mind, miss, recall, regret, relish, remember, repent, resent, (can't) stand, need, bank on, count on, decide on, delight in, play at, resort to, see about, shrink from, go in for, look forward to*

Another class of verbs which show obligatory control are the *commitment* verbs:

(111)   *admit, avoid, confess to, consider, deny, deserve, (can't) help, propose*

Again, in accordance with (109), the committor role of the main verb must be coindexed with the unexpressed subject of the gerund.

So, to return to the contrast between (105a) and (105b), compare the structures they would be assigned under the current analysis:

---

[16]This is slightly simplified; see Pollard and Sag (1994, 296ff) for some complicating factors which are irrelevant to the present discussion.

[17]The verbs in (110), (111), (117), and (126) are the subjectless -*ing* complement-taking verbs in Quirk et al. (1985, 1189).

(112) a.

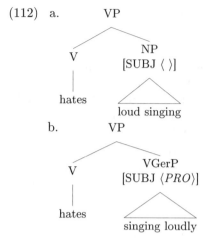

b.

The phrase *loud singing* is a subject-saturated NP, and so (109) does not apply. The PRO-*ing* gerund *singing loudly* is an unsaturated clause, so the reference of the *PRO* subject is governed by the constraint in (109).

This treatment of control can also handle some curious data discussed by McCawley (1988, 139) that would be very difficult to account for under a syntactic analysis of control:

(113)   a. Getting a low grade didn't bother John.
           b. Driving recklessly gives some people thrills.

In these examples, the unexpressed subject of the PRO-*ing* gerund phrase is controlled by some other argument of the main verb. These facts too are amenable to the semantic approach to control outlined in (109). *Bother* and *give thrills to* are *orientation*-class verbs, and as expected the unexpressed subject of the gerund is coindexed with the *experiencer* role of the main verb.[18]

Sag and Pollard's semantic Control Principle also can account for verbs with apparently arbitrary control. One such group is the *influence* class verbs:

(114)   *discourage, forbid, permit, recommend, do away with*

These verbs do not require coreference between their subject (i.e., the *in-fluencer*) and the unexpressed subject of their complement, as in (115a). However, the unexpressed subject of the gerund must be coreferent with the *influenced* role when it is expressed, as in (115b).

---

[18]McCawley also cites examples like *Running away was cowardly of Derek* and *Punching Harry led to Susan's downfall*, which fit less obviously into the semantic taxonomy of (109).

(115) a. The law forbids exposing oneself.
b. The law forbids flashers from exposing themselves.

This follows directly from (109).

Finally, (109) predicts that verbs which do not fall into the *influence, commitment,* or *orientation* classes allow genuinely arbitrary control. Take, for example, these sentences from the Brown corpus (Frances 1964):

(116) a. All four types of message listed in Table 1 are permitted, although decorum and cocktail tradition require holding the commands to a minimum, while exclamations having complimentary intonations are more than customarily encouraged.
b. He reported, too, that among the habitants there were none of probity and ability sufficient to justify entrusting them with the King's goods.

The verbs *involve, require,* and *justify* allow a subjectless gerund complement, but do not seem to put any restrictions on the interpretation of the omitted subject. This follows from the fact that these verbs do not fall into the semantic classes specifically mentioned in (109).

One type of verb which appears to violate (109) is the class of aspectual verbs:

(117)   *cease, commence, continue, quit, resume, start, stop*

These verbs do not fall into any of the semantic classes mentioned, and yet they seem to exhibit obligatory control:

(118) *Leslie stopped nominating oneself.

However, there is some fairly equivocal evidence that these verbs are actually subject raising verbs that combine with a participial VP complement. For one, these verbs do not combine happily with the *-ing* form of the perfect auxiliary *have:*

(119) *Pat resumed having gone to the store.

This would be immediately explained if these verbs select for a present participle rather than a gerund, since perfect *have* lacks the former (Gazdar et al. 1982):

(120) a. *Pat is having gone to the store.
b. Sandy was relieved by Pat having gone to the store.

On the other hand, stative verbs are alleged to lack a present participle but can appear as the complement of the verbs in (117):

(121) a. *After a moment of stage fright, Chris is once again knowing all the questions to Alex Trebek's answers.
 b. ?After a moment of stage fright, Chris resumed knowing all the questions to Alex Trebek's answers.

So, it may well be the aspectual nature of *resume* is semantically incompatible with perfect *have,* and that the ungrammaticality of (119) is not due to syntactic factors at all. Indeed, with a little contextual effort, we can produce a sentence parallel to (119) that sounds considerably better:

(122)??The nicotine patches didn't work. Within a month, Pat resumed having smoked a pack of Marlboros by lunchtime every day.

There is also some evidence that these verbs are in fact raising verbs and not Equi verbs. For example, raising verbs typically allow idiom chunks and expletives as subjects:

(123) a. Tabs seem to be kept on the President.
 b. There seems to be a riot in the park.
 c. It seemed to be snowing into the early morning.

Control verbs, on the other hand, do not allow these 'non-referential' subjects:

(124) a. *Tabs want to be kept on the President.
 b. *There wants to be a riot in the park.
 c. *It wanted to be snowing into the early morning.

The aspectual verbs in (117) seem to fall somewhere in the middle, allowing different kinds of non-referential subjects with varying degrees of awkwardness:

(125) a. ?Tabs continue being kept on the President.
 b. There continued being riots in the park.
 c. It continued snowing late into the early morning.

Finally, there is a group of aspectual verbs that seem to fit into the same semantic class as (117) and show the same kind of control facts, but show no signs of being raising verbs:

(126) *break off, give up, leave off, put off, take up, get around to*

In light of the verbs in (126) and the tenebrous nature of the verbs in (117), I will tentatively conclude that these verbs make up a fourth class of control verbs not covered by (109). The hope would be that further investigation into these semantic classes would reveal underlying generalizations about the nature of control.

This section has been a very sketchy outline of how a theory of complement control might be applied to gerunds. As it stands, it suffers from a major weakness pointed out by Pollard and Sag (1994), namely that the assignment of verbs to each semantic class is strictly intuitive. Without independent tests for semantic type, the predictions of (109) are very difficult to verify. But it should be clear that the analysis of PRO-*ing* gerunds developed in the previous sections is at least compatible with Pollard and Sag's (1994) semantic theory of complement control.

2.3.4   Pied piping

One more property of English verbal gerunds that needs to be accounted for is the pied piping contrast between ACC-*ing* and POSS-*ing* VGerPs discussed in §2.1.3.4. As Malouf (2000) argues, this follows from the fact that the former are clauses while the latter are not. To show how this result is achieved, I will first sketch the HPSG treatment of pied piping developed by Pollard and Sag (1994), Sag (1997) and Ginzburg and Sag (1998).

The basic fact that needs to be accounted for by any treatment of pied piping is shown in (127).

(127)   a.   Who failed the exam?
        b.   Whose roommate's brother's neighbor failed the exam?

In a *WH* question, the left-most constituent must contain a *WH* word, but that *WH* word can be embedded arbitrarily deeply. This dependency is encoded by the non-local feature WH. Question words are marked with a non-empty value for the WH, whose value is a set of interrogative parameters. *WH* words also introduce an interrogative parameter in the STORE of the verb which selects them. All parameters and quantifiers introduced into the STORE then must be retrieved somewhere in the sentence and assigned a scope by a constraint-based version of Cooper storage (Cooper 1983, Pollard and Sag 1994).

Take a sentence like (127a). This is an instance of the construction *wh-subj-inter-cl*, which combines a subject and a head to form an interrogative clause. This construction is subject to the constraint in (128).[19]

---

[19]The contained set difference of two sets ($\doteq$) is the ordinary set difference as long as $Y \subseteq X$. Otherwise it is undefined. Likewise, the disjoint set union of two sets ($X \uplus Y$) is the ordinary set union as long as the two sets are disjoint.

(128) *wh-inter-cl* →

$$\begin{bmatrix} \text{STORE} & \boxed{1} \doteq \boxed{2} \\ \text{PARAMS} & \boxed{2} = \boxed{3} \uplus set \\ \text{HD-DTR} & \left[\text{STORE } \boxed{1} \right] \\ \text{NON-HD-DTR} & \left[\text{WH } \boxed{3} \right] \end{bmatrix}$$

This constraint requires that the subject have somewhere inside it a *WH* word which contributes an interrogative parameter. The presence of a *WH* word somewhere inside the phrase is indicated by the phrase's non-empty WH value. The *WH* word can be anywhere inside the subject, so long as its WH value is passed up to the top of the phrase. In addition, this interrogative parameter must be a member of the PARAMS value of the interrogative clause, and all of the members of the clause's PARAMS value are removed from the store and given scope over the clause.

As first proposed by Ginzburg (1992), the interrogative word *who* is optionally specified for a non-empty WH value, as in (129).

(129) *who* →

$$\begin{bmatrix} \text{LOCAL} & \begin{bmatrix} \text{HEAD} & noun \\ \text{STORE } \{\boxed{1}[\text{ which}(\boxed{2}) \mid \text{person}(\boxed{2})]\} \end{bmatrix} \\ \text{NON-LOCAL} & \left[\text{WH } \{(\boxed{1})\} \right] \end{bmatrix}$$

In addition, the lexical entries for all lexical heads obey the WH Amalgamation Principle in (130).

(130) *word* →

$$\begin{bmatrix} \text{LOCAL} & \left[\text{ARG-ST } \left\langle [\text{WH } \boxed{1}], \ldots, [\text{WH } \boxed{2}] \right\rangle \right] \\ \text{NON-LOCAL} & \left[\text{WH } \boxed{1} \cup \cdots \cup \boxed{2} \right] \end{bmatrix}$$

This constraint ensures that the WH value of a head is the union of the WH values of its arguments. These lexical constraints force the head of any phrase that contains a governed *WH* word to have a non-empty WH value reflecting that fact.

Next, the WH Inheritance Constraint, in (131), ensures that the value of WH gets passed from the head daughter to the mother.

(131) *head-nexus* →

$$\begin{bmatrix} \text{NON-LOCAL} \mid \text{WH} & \boxed{1} \\ \text{HD-DTR} \mid \text{NON-LOCAL} \mid \text{WH} & \boxed{1} \end{bmatrix}$$

Similar constraints amalgamate the STORE value of a word's arguments and pass up the STORE value of a phrase from head daughter.

Finally, to guarantee that only questions contain interrogative words, clauses are subject to the constraint in (132).

(132)   *clause* →

   [NON-LOCAL | WH { }]

This requires all clauses to have an empty WH value. This means that any WH value introduced by the lexical entry of an interrogative word must be bound off by an appropriate interrogative construction, ruling out declarative sentences like *Chris flunked which student.*

These constraints provide a completely general, head-driven account of pied piping in both relative clauses and questions. Consider first the non-gerund examples in (133).

(133)   a.   Whose failure was expected?
        b.   *For whom to fail was expected?

In (133a), *failure* will take on the non-empty WH value of its specifier *whose*. The constraint in (131) passes the WH value of *failure* (that is, an interrogative parameter *whose*) up to the entire phrase *whose failure.* The *WH* subject interrogative clause construction forms the interrogative clause *whose failure was expected?* A similar chain of identities passes up the WH value of *whom* in (133b) to the clause *for whom to fail.* But, this violates (132), and the example is ruled out.

Now it should be clear how this theory of pied piping carries over to the verbal gerund examples in (134).

(134)   a.   I wonder whose failing the exam surprised the instructor.
        b.   *I wonder who(m) failing the exam surprised the instructor.

The structure of these examples is given in Figures 14 and 15.   In (134a), *failing* picks up the WH value of *whose* and passes it up to the phrase *whose failing the exam.* Since this is an example of a POSS-*ing* VGerP, a type of *noun-poss-cx* construction, it is not subject to (132). In (134b), though, the subject of the question is a non-finite head-subject clause, which by (132) must have an empty WH value. This conflicts with both the constraints on WH percolation and with (128), and the sentence is ungrammatical. The difference between POSS-*ing* and ACC-*ing* VGerPs with respect to pied piping follows directly from independently motivated constraints on construction types. Any analysis which treats the subject case alternation as essentially free variation would be hard pressed to account for this difference without further stipulations.

By adapting Ginzburg's theory of interrogatives to Sag's (1997) anal-

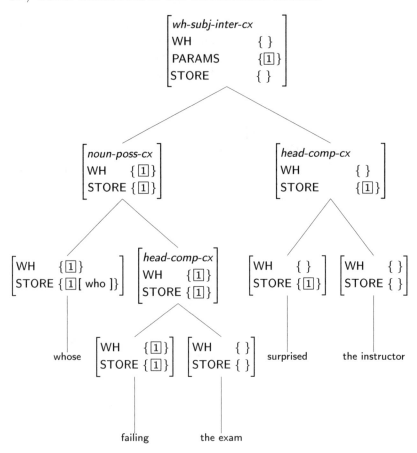

FIGURE 14 *whose failing the exam surprised the instructor?*

ysis of pied piping, we can also account for the behavior of VGerPs in
multiple *WH* questions. For multiple *WH* questions, Ginzburg (1992,
331) suggests "the need for syntactic distinctions between forms that
are, intuitively, interrogative syntactically and semantically and forms
that are declarative syntactically, but have interrogative contents." In
a multiple *WH* question, *WH* words which are left-most in their clause
have both interrogative syntax and interrogative semantics. They pass
up a non-empty WH value in exactly the same way as in ordinary *WH*
questions. *WH* words which are not clause initial, on the other hand,
have only interrogative semantics. While they introduce an interrogative
parameter into the store, they have an empty WH value. This is what
accounts for the non-contrast in (135).

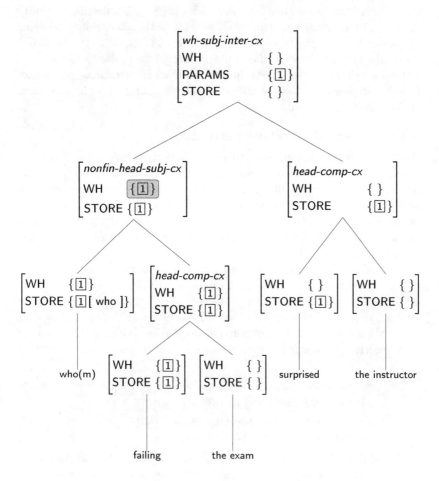

FIGURE 15 *whom failing the exam surprised the instructor?*

(135) a. I wonder who was surprised by whose failing the exam.
       b. I wonder who was surprised by who failing the exam.

The structures of (135) is given Figure 16. Note that I have assumed Pollard and Yoo's (1998) head-driven STORE collection here, but I have crucially not adopted their analysis of multiple *WH* questions. Unlike (134b), (135b) does not run afoul of (132), the constraint requiring clauses to have empty WH values. Since the ACC-*ing* VGerP *who failing the exam* appears in situ, it is only interrogative semantically and its WH value is empty. No constraints prohibit an interrogative parameter from being passed up via the storage mechanism and so both (135a) and (135b) are grammatical.

2.4   Postscript: Archaic gerunds

Diachronic syntactic changes can pose a serious problem to theories of synchronic grammar that presuppose a rigid set of categories. As observed by Lichtenberk (1991), among others, change often proceeds gradually, with a form accruing new properties bit by bit. At the 'end-points' of the change, the old and new forms may fit into clearly defined categories, but the intermediate stages will show a mixture of properties from two different categories.

English verbal gerunds are an example of a form that developed gradually. Verbal nouns and present participles are found in the earliest stages of Old English with properties very similar to those of their modern reflexes. Prior to 1200, the verbal nouns, like Modern English nominal gerunds, had strictly nominal properties, taking a direct object as a genitive possessor or later as a periphrastic possessor marked by *of*:[20]

(136) a. toeacan þæs   landes   sceawunge
           moreover the(GEN) land(GEN) seeing

           'in addition the observing of the land'   (?a890, p. 42)
       b. redunge of englisc oðer of frensch   (?a1200, p. 62)

In the Middle English period, verbal nouns began to show verbal properties. In these examples, the gerunds without determiners take an accusative direct object with no intervening *of:*

(137) a. yn *feblyng þe body* with moche fastyng   (c1303, p. 76)
       b. Yn goyng to þe deþ, he shewed obedyens Yn *fulfyllyng hys faders comoundemens*   (a1325, p. 76)

---

[20]Page numbers are references to Tajima (1985), on whom this discussion of the development of verbal gerunds is primarily based.

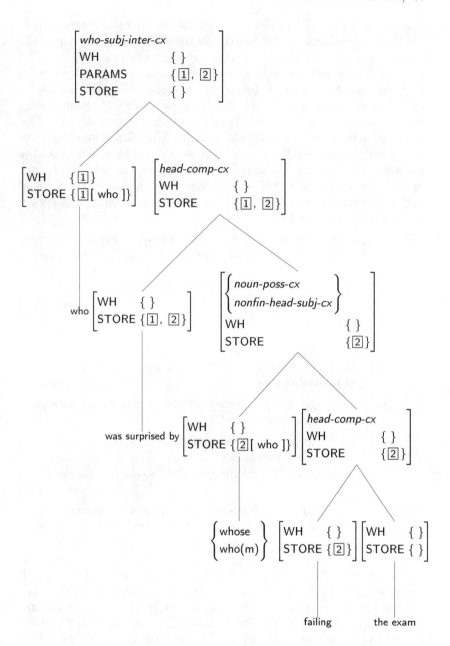

FIGURE 16 *Who was surprised by whose/whom failing the exam?*

This verbalization of the gerund is possibly related to an earlier morphological development. Around the fourteenth century, the participial ending -*nde* and the feminine abstract verbal noun ending -*ung* coalesced to -*ing*. One hypothesis about the development of the verbal gerund is that this new homonomy between the two forms allowed the transfer of verbal properties from the participle to the gerund. Houston (1989), in particular, argues that gerunds gained the ability to take accusative direct objects when they occurred as objects of prepositions, by analogy to functionally similar appositive present participles. Whatever the mechanism of the change, this new verbal character spread to other uses of the gerund. By the end of the fourteenth century, gerunds are found with both verbal properties (accusative objects) and nominal properties (determiners and adjectives):

(138) a. grete remorse I haue in my soule of *the untrewe forgyng and contryvyng certayne testamentys and last wyll* by naked wordes (c1454, p. 81)

b. Hee denies *the bringing the army to London* (Wescoat 1994)

c. the uttering sweetly and properly the conceit of the minde [Sidney]

d. my wicked leaving my father's house [Defoe]

e. the being weighted down by the stale and dismal oppression of rememberance [Dickens]

And, by the fifteenth century, verbal gerunds can be found with both genitive and accusative subjects:

(139) a. þou woldest leue *þy pursuyng crysten pepull,* and aske God mercy wyth a meke hert (a1415, p. 82)

b. an horrybul fyre schall aryse at *þe sonne goyng downe* (a1415, p. 124)

The mechanisms and the chronology of this shift are a matter of considerable scholarly dispute (e.g., Donner 1986). However, the historical details are not immediately important for the point I am trying to make. What is significant is that there was clearly an intermediate stage between the original nominal gerund and the modern verbal gerund which combined with both an accusative object and a definite article. The existence of this intermediate stage is completely consistent with an approach to syntactic categories that takes into account multiple types of syntactically relevant information. In addition, examples like (138d) show that verbal gerunds showing many of the properties of modern POSS-*ing* gerunds could appear with adjectives rather than adverbs.

In the analysis I have presented here, the nature of the gerund's subject, specifier, and complements are controlled independently by the SUBJ, SPR, and COMPS features. On the other hand, the kind of modifier that can occur with a gerund is determined by the position of its head value in the hierarchy in (98) on page 65. So, it not surprising that the verbal gerund lexical rule in (100) differed in its treatment of subjects and complements at different stages of its historical development. In contrast, an analysis which derives the subject, complement, and modification properties of modern verbal gerunds from their status as verbs (at some level) would not necessarily predict the 'partially verbal' gerunds in (138).

The historical development of gerunds shows that the properties of Modern English verbal gerunds are to a certain extent accidental. Any analysis that predicts that mixed nominal/verbal categories will behave like Modern English verbal gerunds is making too strong a prediction and will not be able to account for earlier stages of the language. In the next chapter, however, we will see that the properties of gerunds in English and in other languages are not randomly distributed. The analysis presented in this chapter therefore is making too weak a prediction and will have to revised.

3

Coherent Nominalizations

One cost of the approach presented in the previous chapter is that it introduces a new lexical category which happens to share some properties of nouns and verbs. A criticism that could be raised then is that it does not provide a restrictive theory of mixed categories. For example, Pullum (1991, 790) notes in his conclusion:

> If the analysis given here is on the right track, we would expect to occasionally find other examples of constituents with heterocategorial heads, identifiable by virtue of having all the external syntactic characteristics of one category but internal syntactic characteristics suggestive of some other category. However, contrary to what some have suggested [...] we would not expect to find arbitrary mixtures of syntactic characteristics from different categories in any constituent type. Instead, the phrasal head of some types of phrase may be sharply and consistently of a different type from the type we would expect from the usual effects of the head feature convention.

The present analysis offers no such restrictions. With a slightly different arrangement of types in (98) on page 65 or values in (100) on page 66 one could represent mixed category items with very different properties from English verbal gerunds.

The essential claim of the previous chapter is that traditional syntactic categories like noun and verb have no first-class status and play no role direct role in linguistic theory. Rather, there are several dimensions of categoriality that may vary independently. Major syntactic categories are commonly recurring bundles of properties. A mixed category, like the English verbal gerund, is a construction that has some of the properties of typical members of more than one part of speech. This view of mixed categories is quite different from the standard generative approach to gerunds. It is standardly assumed (see §2.2) that verbal gerunds show mixed nominal/verbal behavior because they consist of a nominal projection which is converted to a verbal projection at some phrasal level. Under this view, each constituent is fully nominal or fully verbal, and there are no truly mixed categories.

The mixed category analysis presented in the previous chapter makes no direct predictions about the cross-linguistic distribution of nominalizations. The lexical rule mechanism is powerful enough to derive words whose behavior is completely unique. Nothing in this approach explains why gerunds always reuse constraints on nouns and verbs. However, "in all languages, [gerunds] involve marking used in either finite clauses or in possessive NPs" (Koptevskaja-Tamm 1993, 64).

Also, nothing in this approach restricts what kinds of noun/verb hybrids can be formed. If one were to make the (highly dubious) assumption that across languages all possible feature values are equally likely, then this analysis predicts that one should find many kinds of mixed categories that in fact do not occur. For example, if we find gerunds like (1a), whose only nominal property is that it takes a possessive subject, we would expect to also find gerunds like (1b), whose only internal nominal property is the inability to directly govern an object.

(1) a. Pat worries about Chris's endlessly watching television.
     b. *Pat worries about Chris endlessly watching of television.

From the standpoint of a mixed category analysis as I have presented it, these two construction types should be equally likely. They both involve a deverbal noun with some combination of noun-like and verb-like lexical properties. Certainly nothing in this analysis rules out a deverbal noun like (1b). Yet as we shall see it turns out that while constructions like (1a) are quite common in the world's languages, constructions like (1b) are either very rare or nonexistent.

On the other hand, it has been argued that change-over analyses do make predictions about the range of nominalization types. As we will see, the non-occurrence of nominalizations like (1b) suggests that the mixed category approach as I have presented it is too liberal and would seem to support arguments for the change-over approach. In this chapter I will review the cross-linguistic variation, evaluate the predictions of the change-over approach both theoretically and empirically, and show how the mixed category analysis should be refined in light of the cross-linguistic data.

3.1   The Deverbalization Hierarchy

English has a range of nominalization types that can be arranged into a cline, with nominalization types lower on the hierarchy showing increasing nominal properties:

(2)   a.   The DA was shocked that Pat illegally destroyed the evidence.
b.   The DA was shocked by Pat having illegally destroyed the evidence.
c.   The DA was shocked by Pat's having illegally destroyed the evidence.
d.   The DA was shocked by Pat's illegal destroying of the evidence.
e.   The DA was shocked by Pat's illegal destruction of the evidence.

All of the phrase types exemplified in (2b–e) have an external distribution which is a subset (though not necessarily a proper subset) of that of an NP headed by a common noun. The nominalized clause in (2a) has many of the internal properties of a finite clause and no internal properties of an NP. The derived nominal in (2e) has all of the internal properties of an NP and none of the internal properties of a finite clause. The other nominalization types fall in between these two poles.

We can differentiate the nominalization types in (2) on the basis of five properties: whether they include a finite verb, whether they take a direct case (i.e., nominative or accusative) subject, whether they allow an adverbial modifier, whether they take a direct case object, and whether they include a regularly inflected verb form.

Of these properties, all but the first and the last have been discussed at considerable length in the previous chapter. The remaining two are different from the others in that they refer to morphological properties of the head of the phrase rather than the phrase's internal or external syntactic distribution. In English, modal verbs only have a finite form, so if a construction admits a modal verb, then it must admit a finite verb. By that criterion, only the first of the constructions in (2) involves a finite verb form:

(3)   a.   The DA was shocked that Pat might have illegally destroyed the evidence.
b.   *The DA was shocked by Pat might having illegally destroyed the evidence.
c.   *The DA was shocked by Pat's might having illegally destroyed the evidence.

    d. *The DA was shocked by Pat's illegal might destroying of the evidence.

    e. *The DA was shocked by Pat's illegal might destruction of the evidence.

Identifying which of these constructions involve a non-finite verb form and which involve a noun form is somewhat more difficult. One morphological property that uniquely identifies nouns is occurrence with the plural suffix -s. By that criterion, only the last construction in (2) involves a noun form:

(4) a. *The DA was shocked that Pat repeatedly destroyeds the evidence.

    b. *The DA was shocked by Pat havings repeatedly destroyed the evidence.

    c. *The DA was shocked by Pat's havings repeatedly destroyed the evidence.

    d. *The DA was shocked by Pat's repeated destroyings of the evidence.

    e. ?The DA was shocked by Pat's repeated destructions of evidence.

But, there is a problem with interpreting these results. While only nouns take plural -s, not all nouns do. In particular, nouns whose reference cannot be easily quantized, such as mass nouns or abstract nouns, do not happily appear in the plural. So, one might argue that any of (4b–d) are ruled out for semantic reasons, especially in light of (4e)'s marginal acceptability.

However, I think a purely semantic account of (4) will be hard to maintain. While the nominal gerund in (4d) cannot appear in the plural, syntactically identical -ing forms can:

(5)   With "Planet News," music meant to accompany readings of Allen Ginsberg's "Wichita Vortex Sutra," Mr. Glass gets going.

In this case, *readings* can only be interpreted in a specialized sense: "Planet News" is intended to accompany formal public performances of Ginsberg's poem and not, for example, to be listened to over headphones while the poem is read silently. *Destroying* has no such specialized meaning, so (4d) is unacceptable. In general, nominal gerunds can only be pluralized if they have a lexicalized sense. It is difficult to see what systematic semantic difference would explain why regular nominal gerunds lack a plural while lexicalized gerunds, often with only a very slightly specialized meaning, do have plurals. This contrast is easily explained, however, if regular nominal gerunds are syntactically common nouns but morphologically verbs, while the lexicalized forms are common nouns all the way.

To return to the task at hand, we can arrange the results as follows and see that a clear pattern emerges:[1]

(6)

	Finite verb	Direct case subject	Adverb modifier	Direct case object	Verbal form
a.	+	+	+	+	+
b.		+	+	+	+
c.			+	+	+
d.					+
e.					

What this suggests is that in the various English nominalization types, nominal and verbal properties are not randomly mixed. Rather, they can be arranged into the implicational hierarchy in (7).

(7)   Finite verb → Direct case subject → Adverb modifier ' Direct case object → Verbal form

Croft (1991), drawing on Comrie (1976) and his own survey of the properties of syntactic categories in diverse languages, observes that a similar pattern comes up in other languages with several nominalization types. For example, he cites the following Quiché sentences:

(8)   a.   (*š-)ux-ātin-naq   arētaq
         (PAST-)1PL.ABS-bathe-PERF when
         'We had already bathed when...'   (Croft 1991, 84f)
      b.   (*š-)at-nu-¢ukūm   arētaq
         (PAST-)2SG.ABS-1SG.POSS-look.for.PERF when
         'I had been looking for you when...'
      c.   či   qa-čap̓-eš-ik
         for 1PL.POSS-speak.to-PASS-NOM
         'in order to speak to us' (lit. 'for our being spoken to')

In (8a), the nominalized verb takes a direct case subject and object, but not tense marking. In (8b), the nominalized verb takes a direct case object but a possessive subject, and in (8c) neither a direct case subject nor a direct case object is allowed.

Quiché nominalization types fit into the same implicational hierarchy as English nominalization types. There is no nominalization type in

---

[1]Note that while this hierarchy is reminiscent of Ross's (1972, 1973a, 1973b) "category squish", there is an important difference in their interpretations. I will use these facts to argue for relations among discrete categories, while Ross used them to argue against the existence of discrete categories in general.

Quiché that takes a direct case subject but not a direct case object. On the basis of this and other evidence, Croft proposes the universal hierarchy in (9).

(9) DEVERBALIZATION HIERARCHY
If a verbal form inflects for tense-aspect-modality like a predicated verb, then it will take subject and object dependents like a predicated verb. If a verbal form takes a subject dependent like a predicated verb, then it will take an object dependent like a predicated verb (Croft 1991, 83).

This generalization is confirmed by Koptevskaja-Tamm's (1993) much more extensive and systematic cross-linguistic survery of nominalization types. Interestingly, the cross-linguistic data does not support including the choice between adverbial and adjectival modification in the hierarchy.

3.2 Explaining the cross-linguistic pattern

While they are generally motivated on language internal grounds, category change-over analyses have an obvious connection to the Deverbalization Hierarchy. Lapointe (1993), Borsley and Kornfilt (2000), and Bresnan (1997) make this link explicitly: they point out that the attested nominalization types correspond to different levels of phrasal nominalization. Consider the structures in (10). In each case, the fully nominal part of the phrase is limited to the contiguous region within the dotted line. Outside the dotted line, the phrase is fully verbal. In (10a), the NP contains a complete verbal projection and so will take tense marking and will take its subject and complements like a verb does. In (10b), the gerund will combine with its subject and complements like a verb does, but since it lacks an S there will be no tense marking. In (10c), the gerund will only combine with its complements like a verb does; the subject will be realized as the specifier of an NP. Finally, in (10d), the gerund is fully nominalized and will show no non-morphological verbal properties.

The explanation for the Deverbalization Hierarchy offered by change-over analyses is that in a mixed projection there must be a single point of articulation dividing the nominal part of the phrase from the verbal part. Different proposals offer different implementations of this constraint. Lapointe attributes it to a constraint on possible phrase types (see §2.2.4.2), while Borsley and Kornfilt derive it from the universal hierarchical order of functional projections, and Bresnan (1997) derives it from general properties of head-sharing. Nevertheless, the insight behind the proposals is the same. Since this line of argument derives the cross-linguistic distribution of gerunds from a condition on possible

(10)   a.

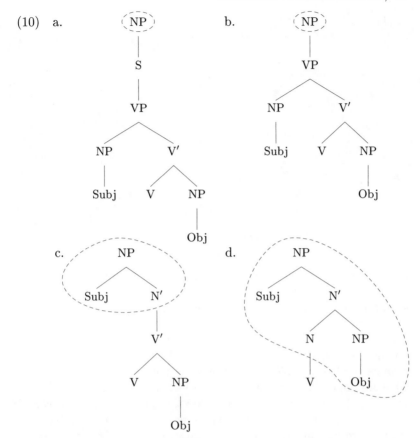

structures, I will call this the **Phrasal Coherence Hypothesis** (PCH). As long as we only allow a single change-over point, the nominalization types in (10) are the only types that are possible. A nominalization that, say, combined with its subject like a verb does but with its complements like a noun does would have to have the structure in (11). In this case, the nominal part of the phrase is split into two regions by an intervening verbal projection, violating the PCH. As long as the PCH is true of all languages, the Deverbalization Hierarchy follows directly from this kind of analysis.

   In contrast to the change-over analyses, the analysis presented in §2.3 does not by itself offer any explanation for the Deverbalization Hierarchy. Under this view, gerunds do not involve any mixed projections. Their hybrid properties follow from their mixed nominal/verbal feature specifications, which in turn are derived in the lexicon. Without

(11)

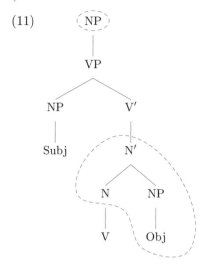

additional constraints on the cross-linguistic distribution of feature values, this analysis predicts that all mixed combinations of feature values should be attested in the world's languages.

Clearly though, not all combinations of feature values are equally likely. Consider an example from the domain of phonology: cross-linguistically sonorant consonants tend to be voiced while obstruent consonants tend to be voiceless (Greenberg 1966b). This is an instance of what we might call local markedness (Tiersma 1982, Croft 1990b). The unmarked value for voicing depends on the manner of articulation. For the sake of discussion, we can represent local markedness via universal Feature Specification Defaults (FSDs) in the style of Gazdar et al. (1985):[2]

(12) a. $\begin{bmatrix} \text{MANNER } \textit{obstruent} \end{bmatrix} \supset \begin{bmatrix} \text{VOICE } - \end{bmatrix}$
  b. $\begin{bmatrix} \text{MANNER } \textit{sonorant} \end{bmatrix} \supset \begin{bmatrix} \text{VOICE } + \end{bmatrix}$

The constraints in (12) should be interpreted to mean that all things being equal, if something is a sonorant, it will be voiced and if something is an obstruent, it will be voiceless. Using this same kind of notation, we can represent the Deverbalization Hierarchy as a pair of local markedness constraints on lexical signs:

(13) a. $\begin{bmatrix} \textit{word} \\ \text{VFORM } \textit{fin} \end{bmatrix} \supset \begin{bmatrix} \text{SUBJ } \langle \textit{synsem} \rangle \end{bmatrix}$

---

[2]I do not mean to imply that FSDs are an especially good way to represent local markedness and I will consider alternative representations in later sections.

b. $\begin{bmatrix} \textit{word} \\ \text{SUBJ } \langle \textit{synsem} \rangle \end{bmatrix} \supset \textit{predicator}$

If a word is finite (i.e., shows the full range of tense/aspect/modality marking), then it selects for a subject like a finite verb does. If a word takes a subject, then it is a predicator. That is to say, it inherits all the constraints on the linking of argument positions to grammatical functions that apply to verbs (Davis 1996, Davis and Koenig 2000).

These markedness constraints are a direct representation of the De-verbalization Hierarchy in an HPSG-style framework. As long as these constraints hold of all words in a language, there could be no lexical entry for a word that, say, has all the morphological possibilities of a finite verb but combines with its subject in the same way that a noun combines with a possessor. Such a word would have a lexical entry that fails to satisfy the implication in (13a), and so would be ruled out. Since this approach derives the Deverbalization Hierarchy from a markedness condition on lexical entries, I will call this position the **Lexical Coherence Hypothesis** (LCH).

3.3 Comparing the PCH and the LCH

At first glance, the PCH may seem clearly superior to the LCH. For languages more or less like English they make more or less the same predictions, and the PCH does so with a simple condition on structures. The LCH, on the other hand, requires FSDs, an additional descriptive device. However, for languages whose structure is rather different from that of English, the predictions made by the two hypotheses diverge. In this section I will discuss several of these cases and show that in each case, the LCH makes the correct predictions and the PCH does not.

3.3.1 Gerunds in VSO languages

One problem with change-over analyses is that the division between the nominal part of the phrase and the verbal part is linked to the hier-archical structure of the phrase. Such analyses predict that all words associated with the nominal part of the phrases should appear outside those associated with the verbal part of the phrase. And, indeed, in many languages (including English) this prediction is borne out. How-ever, it is not clear that this reveals anything about the structure of mixed category constructions cross-linguistically. In SVO and SOV languages, the verb and its object are adjacent, so the phrasal hypothesis and the lexical hypothesis make the same predictions.

When we look at VSO languages, however, the two hypotheses diverge. One such language is Standard Arabic. Arabic has fairly strict noun-possessor order within noun phrases:

(14) a. zur-tu   ?umm-a   r-rajul-i
        visited-I mother-ACC the-man-GEN

        'I visited the man's mother.'   (Fassi Fehri 1993, 223)

    b. *zur-tu   r-rajul-i   ?umm-a
        visited-I the-man-GEN mother-ACC

Any additional nominal modifiers or complements come after the possessor:

(15) a. daxtal-tu daar-a   r-rajul-i   l-waasi^cat-a
        entered-I house-ACC the-man-GEN the-large-ACC

        'I entered the large house of the man.'

                              (Fassi Fehri 1993, 218)

    b. daxtal-tu daar-a   r-rajul-i   l-latii   ḥtaraq-at
        entered-I house-ACC the-man-GEN the-that-F burned-3.F.S

        'I entered the man's house which burned.'

These facts can be accounted for most simply if we assume that in Arabic the noun must combine with its specifier first, before any other dependents, in the order NSO. This would give the NP in (15a) the following structure:

(16)

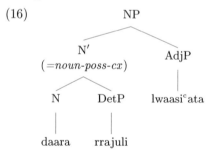

If we assume the verbs also combine with their subjects before their complements, this accounts for the parallel between the NSO order found in noun phrases and the VSO order found in main clauses. However, Borsley (1995) argues against this analysis on the basis of an important difference between noun phrases and clauses.[3] In Arabic clauses, pronominal arguments are expressed via bound pronominal clitics on the verb:

---

[3]Borsley (1995) actually proposes an analysis of Syrian Arabic, which differs from Standard Arabic in crucial ways. The basic argument of this section follows Borsley's, but the examples are Standard Arabic and the final analysis is therefore slightly different. Similar arguments are made for Hebrew by Wintner (in press).

(17) a. *ntaqada   r-rajul-u   ʔiyyaa-hu
         criticized-him the-man-NOM him-ACC
         '(The man criticized him.)'   (Fassi Fehri 1993, 99)
      b. ntaqada-hu   r-rajul-u
         criticized-him the-man-NOM
         'The man criticized him.'

When pronominal, the first object is obligatorily cliticized to the verb. When there is more than one object, cliticization of the second object is optional and slightly dispreferred:

(18) a. ʔaᶜṭay-tu-ka-hu
         gave-I-you-him
         'I gave you him.'   (Fassi Fehri 1993, 106)
      b. ʔaᶜṭay-tu-ka ʔiyyaa-hu
         gave-I-you   him-ACC
         'I gave you him.'

One set of clitics is used for objects and a different set is used for subjects. The form of the subject clitics also varies with the tense and aspect of the verb.

Object clitics are also used for complements of adjectives and prepositions:

(19) a. zayd-un   ḥasan-u   l-wajh-i   wa ʔanta qabiiḥ-u-hu
         Zayd-NOM nice-NOM the-face-GEN and you ugly-NOM-it
         'Zayd has a nice face, and you have an ugly one.'
                                              (Fassi Fehri 1993, 101)
      b. itaqay-tu bi-hi
         met-I   with-him
         'I met him.'

Pronominal arguments in noun phrases are also indicated by clitics on the head noun:

(20) intaqad-tu muʔallif-a-hu
      criticized-I author-ACC-his
      'I criticized its author.'   (Fassi Fehri 1993, 101)

But, interestingly, possessors are indicated by object clitics and the subject clitics are never used. With respect to cliticization, possessors behave like the first complement of a verb. On this basis, Borsley argues that possessors should be treated as complements and noun phrases as head-complement constructions. Object clitics can then be given a uniform analysis. Borsley posits a single lexical rule that removes the first element from the COMPS list of a stem and adds an object clitic:[4]

(21)

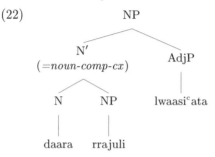

So, the outcome of this digression is that the structure of the Standard Arabic NP is actually as follows:

(22)

This differs from (16) only in the type of construction that the combination of the head noun and the possessor is an instance of.

Returning to the issue at hand, what is potentially troubling for the PCH is that this same NSO order is found in the **maṣdar** construction, comparable to the English POSS-*ing* verbal gerund:

(23) a. ʔaqlaqa-nii ntiqaad-u zayd-in ᶜamr-an
annoyed-me criticizing-NOM Zayd-GEN Amr-ACC
'Zayd's criticizing Amr annoyed me.'

(Fassi Fehri 1993, 223f)

b. *ʔaqlaqa-nii ntiqaad-u ᶜamr-an zayd-in
annoyed-me criticizing-NOM Amr-ACC Zayd-GEN

c. *ʔaqlaqa-nii ᶜamr-an ntiqaad-u zayd-in
annoyed-me Amr-ACC criticizing-NOM Zayd-GEN

Maṣdars behave like any other noun with repsect to cliticization:

(24) a. ʔaqlaqa-nii ntiqaad-u-hu zayd-an
annoyed-me criticizing-NOM-his Zayd-ACC
'His criticism of Zayd annoyed me.'

(Fassi Fehri 1993, 245)

b. *ʔaqlaqa-nii ntiqaad-u-hu zayd-in
annoyed-me criticizing-NOM-his Zayd-GEN

As in (18), the second complement in a maṣdar can be expressed as a clitic, though the free form is slightly preferred:

---

[4]Alternatively, object cliticization could be analyzed as an argument realization alternation, along the lines of Miller and Sag (1997). See §3.4.1 for more discussion.

(25) a. ḍarb-u-ka-hu   ʔaqlaqa-nii
       beating-NOM-you-him annoyed-me
       'Your beating him annoyed me.'   (Fassi Fehri 1993, 106)
    b. ḍarb-u-ka   ʔiyyaahu ʔaqlaqa-nii
       beating-NOM-him your   annoyed-me
       'Your beating him annoyed me.'   (Fassi Fehri 1993, 106)

Again, the most straightforward analysis of this construction is that the maṣdar combines first with its genitive subject, then with its accusative object:

(26)

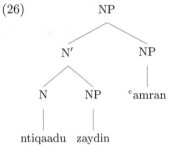

This construction is the same as its English counterpart in many respects. The maṣdar combines with a possessor like a noun does and a complement like a verb does, and the entire phrase has the distribution of an NP. However, unlike the English construction, the verbal part of the phrase is not strictly inside the nominal part.

This problem is even more striking when we look at modification. Maṣdars, like POSS-*ing* verbal gerunds, take adverbial modifiers. In Arabic, modifiers appear after the genitive subject:

(27) ʔaqlaqa-nii ntiqaad-u   r-rajul-i
     annoyed-me criticizing-NOM the-man-GEN
     bi-stimraar-in   haaḏaa l-mašruuᶜ-i
     with-persistence-GEN this   the-project-ACC
     'The man's persistent criticizing of the project annoyed me.'
                                      (Fassi Fehri 1993, 240)

Note that the genitive case marking on *bistimraarin* 'with persistence' is triggered by the adverbial marker *bi-*:

(28) ʔ-uriidu l-intiqaad-a   bi-labaaqat-in
     I-want   the-criticizing-ACC with-courtesy-GEN
     'I want to criticize with courtesy.'   (Fassi Fehri 1993, 239)

According to a change-over analysis, gerunds take adverbial modifiers because they contain a partial verbal projection. This means there must be a verbal projection between the lowest nominal projection (which gives the phrase its nominal specifier) and the highest (which gives the phrase its NP distribution):

(29)

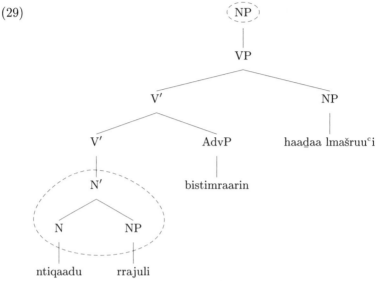

However, that is exactly the structure which is ruled out by the PCH: the nominal part of the phrase is divided into two discontinuous regions.

Under the LCH, though, this is exactly what we would expect to find in a VSO language. Arabic maṣdars can be derived by the following lexical rule, much like its English counterpart:

(30)
$$
\begin{bmatrix} \text{HEAD } verb \\ \text{VAL} \begin{bmatrix} \text{SUBJ} & \langle \boxed{1} \text{NP} \rangle \\ \text{COMPS} & \boxed{2} \\ \text{SPR} & \langle \rangle \end{bmatrix} \end{bmatrix}
\Longrightarrow
\begin{bmatrix} \text{HEAD } maṣdar \\ \text{VAL} \begin{bmatrix} \text{SUBJ} & \langle \rangle \\ \text{COMPS} & \langle \boxed{1} \mid \boxed{2} \rangle \\ \text{SPR} & \langle \rangle \end{bmatrix} \end{bmatrix}
$$

The only difference between this rule and the English gerund rule (100) on page 66 is that in (30) the derived nominal does not select for a subject. Instead, it selects for a possessor as its first complement. This rule derives a word that selects for its complements like the underlying verb does, for its subject like a noun does, and will be modified by adverbs rather than adjectives. Beyond that, the differences between English verbal gerunds and Arabic maṣdars follow from more general differences between the two languages. In English, a noun combines with a possessor via a head-specifier construction, while in Arabic, the possessor is the first complement of a noun.

This is not to say that it is impossible to give an analysis of Arabic maṣdars that is compatible with the PCH. Indeed, Fassi Fehri's analysis of examples like (27) preserves the PCH by assigning maṣdars an underlying SVO structure:

(31)

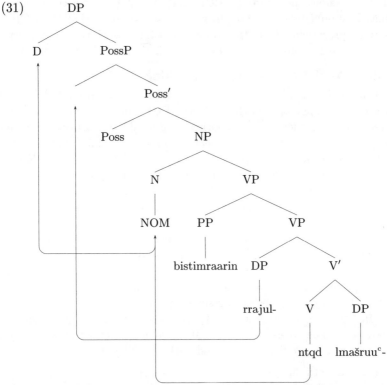

At S-structure, the verb root *ntqd* raises to "support" the abstract nominalizing affix *NOM* and then to D to support the determiner. The subject *rrajul* is either generated in or raises to some position above the modifier, perhaps [Spec, Poss], though why the subject moves and exactly where it lands are left unspecified.

The analysis in (31) gives a contiguous nominal projection at D-structure and the observed surface order at S-structure, but presents problems for the analysis of object clitics. As we have seen in (17b), object clitics in main clauses can raise over an overt subject. In the maṣdar, on the other hand, the object cannot raise over an overt possessor, as shown by (24b). This follows directly from the lexical rule in (30), but must be stipulated under a head-movement analysis (see Fassi Fehri 1993, 246).

The analysis in (31) preserves the PCH, but at considerable methodological cost. The PCH has been proposed by authors working in widely divergent frameworks (e.g., Lapointe (1993) in GPSG, Bresnan (1997) in LFG, Borsley and Kornfilt (2000) in GB), so it may have seemed at first that the choice between the PCH and the LCH was a theory-neutral one. It should be clear though from these examples that the PCH can only be preserved within the context of a framework that makes crucial use of head movement or an equivalent device.

3.3.2 Analytic tense/aspect marking

For languages in which tense, aspect, and modality are indicated by inflectional morphology on the verb, the PCH and the LCH make similar predictions. Under either hypothesis, it would be surprising to find a language which shows tense/aspect marking like a finite verb but whose subject is marked like a possessor. However, for a language that does not mark tense and aspect on the verb, the two hypotheses make divergent predictions. Under the PCH, such languages would be expected to be the same as languages which mark tense and aspect synthetically. On the other hand, verbs in analytic tense-marking languages need not be lexically specified for tense. Since the LCH is a constraint on lexical structures only, it would not rule out a gerund with analytic tense/aspect marking like a main verb and a genitive subject. For at least one language with analytic tense and aspect marking, Boumaa Fijian (Dixon 1988), this seems to be the correct prediction.

In Fijian, a sentence minimally consists of a subject pronoun and a predicate. The reference of the subject can be further specified by an NP within the predicate coindexed with the subject pronoun:

(32) a. era la'o
          3PL go
          'They are going.'   (Dixon 1988, 33)

      b. era la'o a   gone
          3PL go   ART child
          'The children are going.' (lit: 'they are going, the children')
                                                          (Dixon 1988, 33)

A predicate consists of a predicate head (typically a verb) together with its complements and any modifiers. A predicate can also contain particles indicating tense and aspect. These particles come between the subject pronoun and the predicate head:

(33) a. au sa-na   vala gaa   o   yau dua-dua
          1SG ASP-FUT fight MODIF ART 1SG one(REDUP)
          'I'll just fight all by myself.'   (Dixon 1988, 325)

b. au aa   sa taa-niu   oti   i-na   mata'a ni'ua
   1SG PAST ASP chop-copra FINISH in-ART morning today

   'I was cutting copra this morning (and have) completed (the job).'   (Dixon 1988, 73)

The order of elements before the predicate is fixed. The head of the predicate carries no tense/aspect marking or agreement itself.

The structure of an NP in Fijian is parallel to the structure of a clause. An NP minimally consists of an article and a nominal head. Any dependents or modifiers follow the nominal head:

(34) a. a   'oro
        ART village
        'the village'   (Dixon 1988, 35)

     b. a   drau ni pepa yai
        ART sheet of paper this
        'these sheets of paper'   (Dixon 1988, 102)

There are several constructions used to indicate possession, but the most common one places a possessive pronoun between the article and the head of the NP. As with the subject pronoun, the reference of this possessive pronoun can be elaborated by an NP occurring after the head:

(35) a. a   o-na   waqa
        ART CL-3SG boat
        'his/her boat'   (Dixon 1988, 37)

     b. a   o-na   waqa a   cauravou
        ART CL-3SG boat ART youth
        'the youth's boat'   (Dixon 1988, 37)

The classifier prefix o- indicates that the relationship between the head noun and the pronoun is one of ownership or possession.

With the basic structure of clauses and NPs in mind, we are ready to turn to gerunds. A Fijian gerund, or 'clausal NP', consists of an article and a predicate, with the subject of the predicate indicated as if it were the possessor of an NP:

(36) a. o   lesu   mai
        2SG return here
        'You return here.'   (Dixon 1988, 37)

     b. au aa   rai-ca [a   o-mu   lesu   mai]
        1SG PAST see-TR   ART CL-2SG return here
        'I saw your returning here.'   (Dixon 1988, 37)

The range of possibilities for the predicate of a clausal NP is the same as that for the predicate of a main clause. Clausal NPs never include subject pronouns, but beyond that can include anything that a predicate can. This includes the tense and aspect particles:

(37) a. au tadra-a   [a   o-mu aa/na   la'o mai]
     1SG dream-TR ART CL-2SG PAST/FUT go here
     'I dreamt that you had/will come.'   (Dixon 1988, 132)

    b. ... i-na   qou   saa soli-i   au   tale gaa   vei
       in-ART CL.1SG ASP give-TR 1SG again MODIF to
      'emudrau
      2DU
      '(I have told a story) with my giving of myself again to the
      two of you.' (i.e., 'I have given of myself to you two in telling
      the story')   (Dixon 1988, 132)

These are the key examples. The gerunds *la'o* 'go' and *solii* 'give (transitive)' combine with a subject like a noun does but show tense/aspect marking like a main verb, exactly what the Deverbalization Hierarchy leads one to expect will not happen.

The examples in (37) pose a serious problem for the PCH, which is intended as an explanation for the Deverbalization Hierarchy. According to standard GB assumptions, tense and aspect marking is at some level analytic in all languages. Fijian differs from, say, English, in that its tense and aspect markers can stand as independent words and so do not trigger verb raising to Infl. In either case, tense marking is associated with some functional projection higher than the subject at D-structure. So, since the Fijian clausal NP shows tense and aspect marking, it must include a verbal projection higher than the subject. However, since the clausal NP takes a possessive subject pronoun, it must include a nominal functional projection lower than the highest verbal projection. The Fijian clausal NP is a clear violation of the PCH.

There are two ways one might try to avoid this problem. One could assume that the order of functional projections is different in Fijian and English. If in Fijian subjects are associated with a functional projection higher than tense and aspect, then these examples are consistent with the PCH. Alternatively, one could suppose that the subject is generated somewhere lower than IP and then raises to get genitive case. If that were the case, the clausal NP in (37a) would have the structure in (38).

Either alternative, however, fatally weakens any predictive power the PCH might have. The only reason the PCH predicts the Deverbalization Hierarchy is that the order of functional projections is universally fixed

(38)

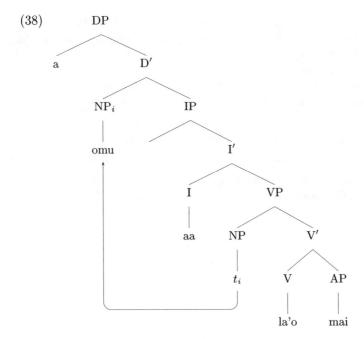

and derivations like (38) are not permitted. If these restrictions are relaxed to allow the apparent violation of the Deverbalization Hierarchy found in Fijian, there is no reason then why violations should not be found in language after language. From the point of view of the PCH, there is nothing special about clausal NPs in Fijian that explains their unusual behavior.

For the LCH, on the other hand, clausal NPs present no problem. The FSD in (13a) is a constraint on lexical entries, and there is no evidence that Fijian verbs are lexically specified for tense or aspect. Indeed, there is no evidence for a contrast between finite and non-finite verbs at all in Fijian.

3.3.3 Mixed word order languages

In all of the languages we have looked at so far (and indeed in most languages of the world) the basic word order of clauses and noun phrases is parallel. That is to say, for example, if the basic word order in clauses is SVO, then the basic word order in noun phrases is PossN, as it is in English. In languages for which this is not the case, however, word order can provide an interesting test for categoriality. If nominalizations contain a verbal projection, then we would expect to see clausal word order. If on the other hand they they contain only nominal projections, then we would expect to see noun phrase word order. On the basis of an extensive survey of nominalization types, Koptevskaja-Tamm (1993, 64) reports that "head dependent word order is the same in [gerunds] and non-derived NPs."

Dagaare is just such a mixed word order language. In Dagaare, complements of finite verbs follow the head:

(39) Nangkpaana da   teɛn-ɛ   la   o   gmɔrfɔ
     Hunter   PAST load-IMP FACT his gun

     'Hunter was loading his gun.'   (Bodomo 1997, 80)

Complements of nominalized verbs, however, precede the head. As we see in (40), Dagaare nominalizations are very similar to English gerunds, with the interesting difference that they allow both adverbial modification and a limited kind of adjectival modification.

(40) a   dɛre   ga-ma   wiewie velaa sɔr-oo   nyɛ
     DEF NAME book-PL quickly good read-NOM this

     'This nice way of Dere's reading books quickly.'
                                                 (Bresnan 1997, 8)

Dagaare has no special case marking on possessors, but since this construction can occur with a determiner in place of a subject, it is more like the English POSS-*ing* gerund than the ACC-*ing* gerund:

(41) a. Bayuo saao di-iu   veɛlɛ   la
         Bayuo food eat-NOM be.good FACT
         'Bayou's eating of the food is good.'
                                                 (Bodomo 1997, 123)

     b. Bayuo gan   wa   veɛlɛ
         Bayuo book NEG good
         'Bayou's book is not good.'

     c. a   saao di-iu   wa   baare
         the food eat-NOM NEG finish.PERF
         'The eating of the food is not yet finished.'
                                                 (Bodomo 1997, 123)

As we would expect, tense and aspect marking is not permitted.

In gerund phrases, like noun phrases, the complements of the nominalized verb precede the head of the phrase. Since the adverbial modifier *wiewie* 'quickly' falls between the nominal head and its complements, this construction would seem to pose a serious problem for the PCH:

(42)

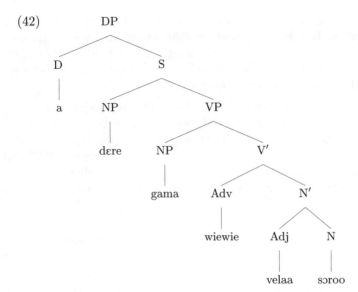

However, Bresnan (1997) argues that Dagaare nominalizations have the head sharing structure in (43), which is consistent with the PCH.

(43)

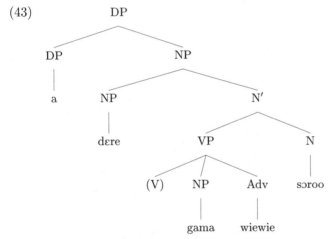

Bresnan proposes to treat mixed categories via functional rather than structural head sharing. The nominalization sɔroo 'reading' has only a single c-structure position, as head of the NP. But, its f-structure is identical to that of the head of the VP. So, under this analysis, the nominalized verb sɔroo 'reading' heads both a nominal projection and a verbal projection. Bresnan goes on to argue that Dagaare nominal-izations are in fact inconsistent with the LCH. She observes that under the head-sharing analysis, *gama* 'books' and *wiewie* 'quickly' form a constituent, while under the more straightforward analysis in (42) they do not. So, she argues, the head-sharing analysis predicts that (44a) should be grammatical, while a lexicalist mixed category analysis falsely predicts that (44b) should be grammatical.

(44) a. a   [daa wiewie] ne [koɔ   gborɔgborɔ] nyu-u
          DEF beer quickly and water frequently   drink-NOM
          'the drinking beer quickly and water frequently'
                                                              (Bresnan 1997, 10)

    b. *a   daa [wiewie nyu-u   ] ne [gborɔgborɔ
          DEF beer   quickly drink-NOM   and   frequently
          dog-oo   ]
          brew-NOM
          'the drinking quickly and brewing frequently beer'
                                                              (Bresnan 1997, 10)

However, it is difficult to see how this poses a problem for the LCH. First, the essential difference between (42) and (43) is not really the constituent structure. A binary branching structure, as in (45), would be consistent with a head-sharing analysis.

(45)

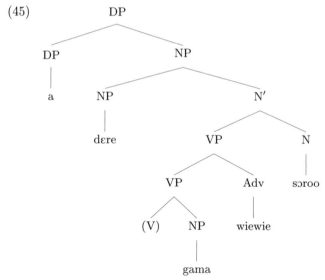

And, a flat structure, as in (46), would be consistent with a purely lexical account of mixed categories. All (44) shows is that there is no constituent that includes the gerund and its modifiers but excludes its complement.

(46)

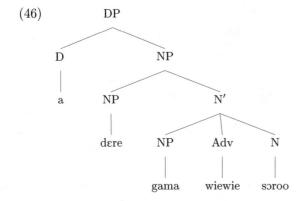

The real difference between the two analyses is the lexical category of the head of the constituent containing the direct object. Suppose, as Bresnan (1997, 10) does, that "apparent conjunction of nonconstituents can be explained by peripheral ellipsis from larger conjoined constituents." Under the head-sharing analysis, then, the constituent structure of (44a) would be:

(47)

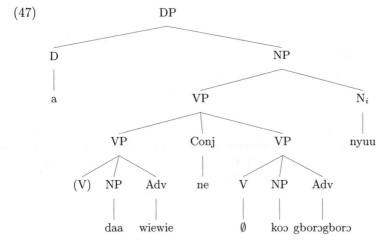

Given the analysis presented here, the structure would be as in (48). So, the real question is whether the constituent containing the direct object and the adverb is like a verb phrase (and therefore head initial) or like a noun phrase (and therefore head final).

Two kinds of evidence suggest that the conjoined phrases in (44) are noun phrases and not verb phrases. First, Dagaare has several coordinating conjunctions. The conjunction *a* 'and' is used for joining verbal

(48)

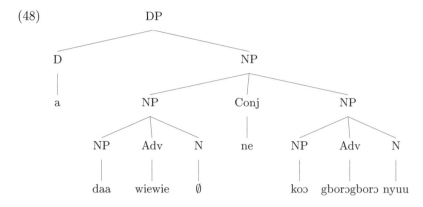

projections:

(49) Badɛre da   gaa-ɛ   la   a   te   mii   tangma   a
      Spider PAST go-PERF FACT and DIR shake sheafruits and
      leɛ   kul   wa   zeng a   di-re
      return go.home come sit and eat-IMP
      'Spider went and gathered sheafruits and came back home and
      was sitting there eating.'   (Bodomo 1997, 128)

The conjunction *ane* or *ne* is used for joining nominal projections:

(50) Bayuo ane Ayuo ane Pɔgdaa gaa   la   sakuuri
      Bayuo and Ayuo and Pogdaa go.PERF FACT school
      'Bayuo and Ayuo and Pogdaa went to school.'
                                          (Bodomo 1997, 129)

The gerund phrases in (44) are joined with the nominal coordinator *ne*
and not the verbal coordinator *a*. This would be hard to explain if the
structure of (44a) is (47). However, this is exactly what we would expect
if the structure of (44a) is in fact (48).

    A second possible piece of evidence comes from serial verb construc-
tions. In a Dagaare serial verb construction, the direct object of the
verbs in the verb cluster may either appear after the entire verb cluster,
as in (51a), or it may appear within the verb cluster, as in (51b).

(51) a. ba   zo   gaa   di la   bondirii
          they run.PERF go.PERF eat FACT food
          'They ran there and ate food.'   (Bodomo 1997, 112)
      b. Ayuo da   de   la   a   bie   zegle
          Ayuo PAST take.PERF FACT DEF child seat.PERF
          'Ayuo seated the child.'   (Bodomo 1997, 108)

When serial verb constructions are nominalized, however, the word order is fixed. The shared direct object must come before the verb cluster:

(52) a. a   saao wiewie zo gaa di-iu
          the food quickly go run eat-NOM
          'running there in order to eat the food quickly'
                                        (Bodomo 1997, 125)
      b. *a wiewie zo gaa saao diiu
      c. *a wiewie zo saao gaa diiu

It difficult to know exactly what to make of this fact without a deeper understanding of the source of the variation in (51). But, it does suggest that the direct objects of nominalized verbs in Dagaare are more like nominal complements than they are like the direct objects of finite verbs. This contrast follows naturally from an analysis like (48), while an analysis like (47) would require additional stipulations to rule out (52b–c).

3.3.4   Mixed modifiers

Another language that has been argued to to provide evidence in favor of the PCH is Italian. The *infinito sostantivato* construction (described by Zucchi 1993) is like the English gerund in many respects. It can take adverbs and accusative objects, like a verbal gerund, or it can take adjectives and PP objects, like a nominal gerund:

(53) a. il   mormorare   sommesso/*sommessamente del   mare
          the whisper(INF) soft/*softly   of.the sea
          'the sea's soft whispering'
      b. il   suo mormorare   *sommesso/sommessamente parole
          the his whisper(INF) *soft/softly   words
          dolci
          sweet
          'his softly whispering sweet words'

What is interesting about this construction is that the verbal type can also appear with a prenominal adjective:

(54) il   suo continuo mormorare   parole dolci
      the his continual whisper(INF) words sweet
      'his continutally whispering sweet words'

However, it cannot occur with a post-nominal adjective:

(55) a. *il suo mormorare parole dolci continuo
      b. *il suo mormorare continuo parole dolci

The first example in (55) is ruled out on general grounds because attributive adjectives in Italian must be adjacent to the head they modify.[5] This is true even for common nouns:

(56) a. *la distruzione del villaggio efferata
       the destruction of.the town cruel
       'the cruel destruction of the town'
    b. la distruzione efferata del villaggio
       the destruction cruel of.the town

Bresnan (1997) argues that under the PCH, the example in (55b) is also ruled out on general grounds. Given this view, an example like (54) would have something like the following structure:

(57)

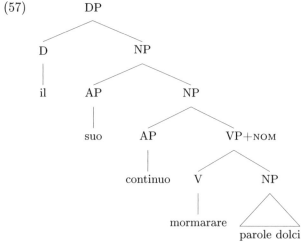

In this structure, the region of the phrase to the right of *mormarare* 'to whisper' is part of a verbal projection, while the region to the left is part of a nominal projection. Therefore, one would expect to find adverbs to the right of the head and adjectives to the left.

On the other hand, the LCH by itself imposes no constraints on the positions that modifiers should be able to appear in. Whether a nominalization takes adjectival modifiers, adverbial modifiers, or both is determined by the position of its HEAD value in the hierarchy of lexical categories (see (98) on page 65). If a nominalization allows both adverbial and adjectival modifiers, the LCH makes no predictions about the relative order of the modifiers.

So, it would appear that the LCH misses an important generalization that the PCH captures. However, this is true only if lexical coherence is

---

[5] For a discussion of apparent exceptions to this generalization, see Cinque (1994).

the only constraint on gerunds. Clearly, however, gerund phrases obey the same syntactic constraints as other constructions. The combinatoric potential of a gerund as expressed by the information in its lexical entry must be realized phrasally by means of the constructions available in the language. These constructions then impose further constraints on the distribution and behavior of gerund phrases. For example, it was argued in §2.3.4 that the differences in pied piping between ACC-*ing* and POSS-*ing* verbal gerund in English follow from general differences between the constructions which they are instances of. In the case of the Italian infinito sostantivato, the distribution of adjectives and adverbs also follows from general constraints on modifier constructions.

First, adverbs in Romance languages generally do not precede the VP they modify (see Pollock 1989). Instead, they appear after the head verb:

(58) a. Gianni rovesciò velocemente il   suo caffè
Gianni dropped quickly   the his coffee
'Gianni quickly dropped his cup of coffee.'
(Crisma 1993, 71)

b. Stanley ha completemente mangiato i   Wheaties
Stanley has completely   eaten   his Wheaties
'Stanley completely ate his Wheaties.'

So, one would not expect adverbs to appear before the head in the infinito sostantivato either. No additional constraints are required to rule out prenominal adverbs.

Second, prenominal adjectives in Italian have a very special status. The alternation between prenominal and postnominal adjectives is not simply a matter of word order variation. As has long been observed, some adjectives are restricted to appear in post-nominal position:

(59) a. Un'infezione batterica
an infection bacterial
'a bacterial infection'   (Crisma 1995, 59)
b. *Una batterica infezione

Other adjectives are only permitted in prenominal position:

(60) a. La mera menzione del   nome del   fratello ha
the mere mention   of the name of the brother has
infastidito Gianni
annoyed   Gianni
'The mere mention of his brother's name annoyed Gianni.'
(Crisma 1995, 60)

b. *La menzione mera del nome del fratello ha infastidito Gianni

A third class of adjectives can occur in either position, but with two different meanings:

(61) a. Il mio povero cugino è stato messo in prigione
the my poor cousin is been put in jail
'My wretched cousin was jailed.'   (Crisma 1995, 60)
b. Il mio cugino povero è stato messo in prigione
the my cousin poor is been put in jail
'My indigent cousin was jailed.'

Finally, the majority of adjectives can appear in either position with more or less the same meaning:

(62) a. la loro brutale aggressione all'Albania
the their brutal agression to the Albania
'their brutal aggression against Albania'
(Cinque 1994, 88)
b. la loro aggressione brutale all'Albania
the their agression brutal to the Albania

However, even for relatively free adjectives, there is a subtle difference in meaning. The postnominal adjective receives a restrictive manner interpretion, while the prenominal adjective has a subject-oriented reading (in the sense of Jackendoff 1972). As Cinque (1994, 89) puts it:

[(62a)] can be paraphrased as: "It was brutal of them to attack Albania" (even though the way they did it could well have been non brutal). [(62b)] on the other hand is only compatible with a situation in which the manner of the aggression was brutal.

This difference is subtle, but is further underlined by the following contrast:

(63) a. Le aggressioni brutali vanno severamente condannate
the aggressions brutal must severly   be.condemned
'Brutal aggressions must be severely condemned.'
(Cinque 1994, 89)
b. *Le brutali aggressioni vanno severamente condannate

In this case, since there is no subject, only the postnominal manner adjective is acceptable.

In addition to the subject-oriented reading, Crisma (1993, 1995) argues that prenominal adjectives can also get a 'speaker-oriented' reading.

For example:

(64) a. L'evidente provocazione di Gianni
the evident provocation of Gianni

'Gianni's evident provocation'(=it is evident that Gianni is
provoking somebody) (Crisma 1993, 75)

b. La provocazione evidente di Gianni
the provocation evident of Gianni

'Gianni's evident provocation'(=Gianni is provoking somebody in a manifest way)

In these examples, the postnominal adjective is a restrictive modifier
while the prenominal adjective is indicating the speaker's evaluation of
the situation.

Whatever the precise characterization of the semantics of prenominal adjectives is, both (62) and (64) show that the prenominal position
itself carries a particular meaning. Adjectives like *batterico* 'bacterial' in
(59), which are incompatible with this meaning, cannot appear prenom-
inally, while other adjectives get a different interpretation by virtue of
appearing in this position. This suggests that prenominal adjectives are
not simply adjoined to the head noun, but are licensed by a specialized
construction, an analysis further supported by the fact that only a single
prenominal adjective is permitted:

(65) la probabile *(e) naturale reazione de sdegno
the probable and natural reaction of distain

Exactly what the status of this construction is is a matter of some de-
bate (see, e.g., Valois 1991, Bernstein 1993, Crisma 1993, Cinque 1994,
Menuzzi 1994, Crisma 1995, Allegranza 1998). However, the consensus
seems to be that prenominal adjectives are somehow associated with
the determiner system, perhaps as heads or specifiers of some functional
projection between the noun and the determiner.

One thing that is clear is that however this construction is represented, it is less restrictive in what it allows to be modified than the
regular head-modifier construction. For example, it allows adjectival
modification of proper names:

(66) a. La sola Maria si è presentata
the alone Maria showed up

'Only Maria showed up.' (Longobardi 1994, 625)

b. ?La Maria sola si è presentata
the Maria alone showed up

'The Maria who is (notoriously) alone showed up.'

A postnominal adjective modifying *Maria* is only marginally acceptable, and then only contrastively to pick out a particular Maria from a set of people named Maria. And, apparently, this construction licenses a prenominal adjective with a nominalized head in the infinito sostantivato, as we saw in (54).

So, the conclusion to draw is that Italian gerunds behave pretty much like their English counterparts. They are modified by adverbs which, like all adverbs in Italian, appear after the head they modify. However, unlike English, Italian has an additional construction which allows a single adjective to appear between the determiner and the head in an NP, and this construction allows an adjective to modify a gerund. The distribution of modifiers in the infinito sostantivato follows from independently motivated constraints, and nothing about the grammar of Italian suggests that either example in (55) should be grammatical. Since there is no need to invoke the PCH to explain the their failure to be acceptable, the LCH and the PCH make the same predictions in this case.

3.4 Deriving the LCH

It should be clear now that a constraint on possible lexical entries can account for the cross-linguistic distribution of gerunds as well as, if not better than, a constraint on possible phrasal configurations. However, as I have pointed out, nothing in the analysis presented in §2.3 actually provides such a constraint on lexical entries. The main problem with this analysis as I have presented it is that too much information is stipulated in the Gerund Formation Lexical Rule, repeated here:

$$
(67) \quad
\begin{bmatrix}
\text{HEAD} & \begin{bmatrix} verb \\ \text{VFORM} \ prp \end{bmatrix} \\
\text{VALENCE} & \begin{bmatrix} \text{SUBJ} & \langle \boxed{1}\text{NP} \rangle \\ \text{COMPS} & \boxed{2} \\ \text{SPR} & \langle \, \rangle \end{bmatrix}
\end{bmatrix}
\implies
\begin{bmatrix}
\text{HEAD} & gerund \\
\text{VALENCE} & \begin{bmatrix} \text{SUBJ} & \langle \boxed{1} \rangle \\ \text{COMPS} & \boxed{2} \\ \text{SPR} & \langle \boxed{1} \rangle \end{bmatrix}
\end{bmatrix}
$$

In this section I will outline how this rule could be refined to avoid any unnecessary stipulations.

3.4.1 The semantic basis for syntactic categories

Suppose every lexeme is classified along three dimensions, according to linking, realization, and category properties, as in Figure 17. Linking types specify the relationship between semantic roles and argument structure positions, realization types specify the relationship between argument structure and grammatical relations, and category types specify

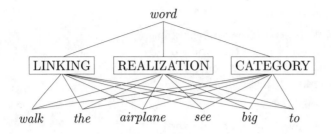

FIGURE 17   A three-way classification of lexems

the relationship between head value and semantic type.

The first two dimensions in Figure 17 are familiar from much earlier work in virtually all syntactic theories. Within HPSG, linking has been explored in depth by Wechsler (1995), Davis (1996), and Davis and Koenig (2000). The realization dimension has received less attention in the HPSG literature, but it is no less important. Pollard and Sag (1994) assume that realization is trivial, that is, that at least for verbs the first element on the argument structure is always the subject and any remaining arguments are complements. More recently, efforts have turned to exploring alternative realization possibilities: Miller and Sag (1997) and Abeillé et al. (1998a) propose that French allows certain arguments to be realized either as complements or as clitics, and Bouma et al. (in press) analyze long-distance dependency constructions as a realization alternation.

So, semantic roles are associated with positions in an abstract syntactic argument structure, which are in turn realized as elements in the 'surface' syntax. Each of these associations allows a certain amount of variation but is constrained by general principles. So far, this model of the lexicon should be fairly uncontroversial. While the details are sometimes hotly contested, in its general outline this is the picture that has emerged as a standard view in HPSG and in many other frameworks as well (e.g., Gerdts 1992, Chomsky 1993, Bresnan 1995, Jackendoff 1997).

The third dimension, category, is more controversial. In fact, it is commonly assumed that there is no regular association between semantic types and lexical categories. Langacker (1987b) cites Langacker (1973, 87) as warning "...no constant semantic effect is associated with the functioning of a morpheme as a noun, as a verb, or as any other part of speech."

In contrast, traditional grammars and modern school grammars assume a semantic characterization of the parts of speech. For example, *Schoolhouse Rock* (Yohe and Newall 1996) offered the following musical definitions of nouns:

> Well, every person you can know,
> And every place that you can go,
> And anything that you can show,
> You know they're nouns.

and of verbs:

> I get my thing in action (Verb!)
> In being, (Verb!) In doing, (Verb!)
> In saying
> A verb expresses action, being, or state of being.
> A verb makes a statement.
> Yeah, a verb tells it like it is!

As it stands, though, this is clearly inadequate. Not all nouns denote a person, place, or thing; some nouns denote an action or "state of being". The best we can say is that *typical* nouns and *typical* verbs can be characterized semantically. Generative grammar, unable to make reference to 'typical' members of categories, has therefore taken it as an axiom that the parts of speech can only be defined extensionally.[6] In the generative tradition being a noun means being marked [+N, −V], nothing more and nothing less.

Despite its shortcomings, the traditional semantic classification is quite attractive. It seems obvious that meanings are not randomly distributed across word classes. Furthermore, in light of work in prototype theory, the shortcomings of the traditional approach to word classes can be seen as shortcomings of the classical Aristotelean approach to categories and classification in general (Lakoff 1987, Taylor 1995). While it is not possible to state necessary and sufficient semantic conditions for nounhood, that does not mean the class of nouns has no semantic coherence.

It has long been recognized that not all categories can be defined in terms of common properties. Wittgenstein (1953) famously argued against the possibility of coming up with a set of defining criteria for a simple category like *game*. While there are no properties shared by all games, games as a class share a number of family resemblances. Later, in a series of well-known experiments, Rosch (1973, 1978) showed that people's conception of categories does not match the classical model but

---

[6]A notable exception is Emonds (1987, 37), who suggests "...we could associate the plus values of Chomsky's features with a reference-generating material 'perturbation' on an essentially innate Kantian space-time perceptual grid." Grimshaw (1981) and Pinker (1982) also discuss the relationship between syntactic and semantic categories. We will return to their proposals in §4.2.1.

instead show prototype effects. People perceive some things as being better instance of a category than others. For example, while both apples and tomatoes are technically fruits, for most North Americans an apple is a much better example of a fruit than a tomato is. Furthermore, some levels of categorization in the middle of a hierarchical taxonomy are more salient than others. Further classes are constructed via generalization or specialization from these basic level categories.

Croft (1991) proposes that syntactic categories are prototypical pairings of semantic type and pragmatic function. Croft proposes three basic universal semantic types (*action*, *object*, and *property*) and three pragmatic functions (*predication*, *reference*, and *modification*). Croft's notion of semantic type corresponds well with the HPSG notion of semantic type. Croft's types are slightly different from, say, Davis's, but they are in principle compatible. Pragmatic functions are more or less what Searle (1969) called propositional acts: "referring indicates what one is talking about, predicating indicates what is being said about it, and modifying indicates a secondary referring or predicating function (restrictive and non-restrictive modification respectively)" (Croft 1990a, 248).

On the basis of a survey of twelve languages (along with informal observation of many more), Croft goes on to argue for the following three universal syntactic categories:

(68)   Verb   Action   ⟷   Predication
        Noun   Object   ⟷   Reference
        Adjective   Property   ⟷   Modification

This is not to say that other associations cannot exist. The claim is only that these associations are prototypical. The prediction is that non-prototypical associations will be structurally or behaviorally marked, and that:

> ... nonprototypicality involves an "unnatural" or at least "imperfect" correlation of lexical semantic root with syntactic construction (referring expression, predication, attribution). In those cases, there will be a mixture of properties, some associated with the syntactic category expressed and some associated with the syntactic construction that the lexical semantic root is naturally correlated with. (Croft 1991, 100)

In HPSG terms, pragmatic functions would have to be associated with types of constructions. Clausal constructions are used for predicating and certain head-specifier constructions are used for referring. However, the categories in (68) are *lexical* categories. The link between a word and the constructions it can be a part of is its HEAD value. A partial hierarchy of HEAD values is given in (69).

(69)

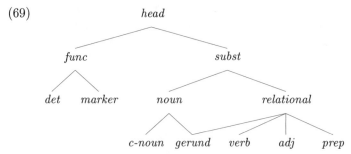

In this context, *c-noun* corresponds to Croft's *reference* and *verb* is Croft's *predication*. A straightforward way to express Croft's basic insight in the context of an HPSG lexical hierarchy is as pairings of a semantic type with a head type:

(70)   a. $v \rightarrow$

$$\begin{bmatrix} \text{HEAD } verb \\ \text{CONT } psoa \end{bmatrix}$$

       b. $n \rightarrow$

$$\begin{bmatrix} \text{HEAD } c\text{-}noun \\ \text{CONT } nom\text{-}obj \end{bmatrix}$$

The content type *psoa* stands for 'parameterized state of affairs' in the situation theoretic sense (Barwise and Perry 1983), and corresponds to Croft's *action*, and the content type *nom-obj* corresponds to Croft's *object*.[7]

However, the constraints in (70) only capture half of Croft's claim: categories are not just associations of meaning and function, they are *prototypical* associations of meaning and function. Without a notion of prototype, this classification is either as easily falsified as the traditional semantic classification, or it is as empty of predictive power as the generative classification.

3.4.2   Prototypes in the lexical hierarchy

How then do we represent prototypicality in the HPSG lexical hierarchy? A standard HPSG type hierarchy is essentially a classification by schema, where a schema is "an abstract characterization that is fully compatible with all the members of the category it defines" (Langacker 1987a, 371).

---

[7]Although the meaning of this should be intuitively clear, an exact characterization of the semantic poles of (70) is hard to come by (see, e.g., Langacker 1987b, Anderson 1997).

Langacker goes on to compare schemas with prototypes:

> Whether by schema or by prototype, categorization resides in a comparison event of the form $S > T = V$. It is achieved when the conceptualizer succeeds in observing in the target (T) a configuration that satisfies some or all of the specifications of the standard (S). More precisely, V—the magnitude of the discrepancy between the standard and the target—is required to fall below a certain threshold of tolerance. When all the specifications of S are satisfied by T, so that $V = 0$, S is referred to as a schema, and the categorizing relationship $S \rightarrow T$ is of one elaboration or specialization... When there is some inconsistency between S and T, so that V has a nonzero value, S can be referred to as a prototype, in a generalized sense of the term; the categorizing relationship $S \Rightarrow T$ then involves extension rather than simple elaboration...

A monotonic type hierarchy is a special case of what Langacker calls a schematic network, one that includes only elaboration links and in which the 'elaborates' relation is transitive. To generalize our type hierarchy to represent prototypicality then all we need to do is to introduce extension links, i.e., to allow default inheritance (Lascarides and Copestake 1999).[8] The constraints in (70) can be rewritten as defaults, as in (71).

(71) a. $v \rightarrow$

$$\begin{bmatrix} \text{HEAD} \ / \ verb \\ \text{CONT} \ psoa \end{bmatrix}$$

   b. $n \rightarrow$

$$\begin{bmatrix} \text{HEAD} \ / \ c\text{-}noun \\ \text{CONT} \ nom\text{-}obj \end{bmatrix}$$

In a default constraint, feature values marked with '/' can be overridden by conflicting constraints on more specific types. All things being equal, objects of type v will be constrained to have a HEAD value of type *verb*. Some subtype of v however could impose a conflicting constraint, say that the HEAD value be an object of type *gerund*. Rather than creating an inconsistency, this additional constraint overrides the default information in (71a).

---

[8]Default unification as defined by Lascarides and Copestake (1999) is a binary, order independent deterministic operation, and so does not suffer from the same theoretical or practical problems usually associated with defaults (see Lascarides et al. 1996).

While the constraints in (71) resolve one problem, they introduce another: they place no restrictions on non-prototypical categories. Nothing rules out a subtype of v with a head value of *det*, for example. This is a common objection to prototype theories of classification in general (e.g., Osherson and Smith 1981). Essentially, anything with a *psoa* content could be a member to some degree of the category whose prototypical members meet the constraint in (71a). Clearly this is undesirable.

We can avoid this difficulty by adding additional non-default constraints to the default constraints in (71):

(72) a. $v \rightarrow$

$$\begin{bmatrix} \text{HEAD } relational \ / \ verb \\ \text{CONT } psoa \end{bmatrix}$$

  b. $n \rightarrow$

$$\begin{bmatrix} \text{HEAD } noun \ / \ c\text{-}noun \\ \text{CONT } nom\text{-}obj \end{bmatrix}$$

Any more specific constraints that override the defaults in (72) must still satisfy the hard constraints in (72). By default the head value of a word of type v is of type *verb*, but no matter what its head value must be compatible with *relational*. Recall that adverbs modify *relational* phrases. Thus (72a) is consistent with the intuition (discussed in §3.1) that there is a connection between adverbial modification and event-denoting semantics.

Default inheritance as appealed to by, e.g., Sag (1997), is an abbreviatory device that helps simplify the construction of lexical type hierarchies. When used in this way, defaults add nothing essential to the analysis. They simply provide a mechanism for minimizing the number of types required. Any type hierarchy that uses defaults can be converted into an empirically equivalent one that does not use defaults, but is perhaps undesirable for methodological reasons. Either way, the constraints that ultimately are inherited by phrasal and lexical constructions are the same.

What I am proposing here is a rather different use of defaults. If default inheritance is used to model extension from a prototype, then two hierarchies that yield the same set of lexical constraints via a different arrangement of types would be substantively different. Different hierarchies implicitly make different claims about the prototypicality of certain constraints, and claims about prototypicality have empirical consequences. So rearranging a type hierarchy to eliminate defaults actually results in a theory that makes different predictions.

Following Greenberg (1966a), Croft (1991) identifies several morphosyntactic criteria for identifying marked and unmarked forms. These properties follow more or less directly from a hierarchical representation of prototypes.

For example, Croft points out that "an unmarked form will display at least as great a range of grammatical behavior as the marked form" (56). By definition, less marked types in the hierarchy are less specific than more marked types. In addition, the constraints on a more marked type must be at least as specific as the constraints on a less marked type. Marked forms, which are of a more specific type and which are subject to potentially more specific constraints, will naturally occur in more specific environments. Related is Croft's observation that "in text counts, the unmarked value will be at least as frequent as the marked value." Again, forms subject to less specific constraints will be able to occur in more discourse contexts. If we assume that, on average, discourse contexts are equally likely, unmarked constructions will be found more frequently.

Default inheritance provides a convenient way to model prototypicality in a lexical type hierarchy. In a narrow sense, every non-maximal type (that is, every type that has at least one subtype) is a prototype with respect to its subtypes. In a more general sense, we can say that the more subtypes a type has, the greater its prototypicality. What we cannot explain yet is the connection between prototypicality and productivity. Nothing so far accounts for the fact that the prototype in effect provides a template for new members of a class.

As it is usually presented (e.g., Pollard and Sag 1987), the HPSG hierarchical lexicon is completely closed: all lexical types are explicitly listed and located within the type hierarchy. However, as Koenig and Jurafsky (1994), Koenig (1994), Koenig (1999b), and Smets (1999) observe, such type hierarchies make it difficult to model productivity. In a closed hierarchy, every type is listed, whether or not its existence is predictable. Since no distinction is made between irregular types and regular types that follow a productive pattern, one must appeal to some external mechanism to explain why it is that new types, with a few interesting exceptions (Pinker 1998), always get assimilated to the regular pattern. Koenig and Jurafsky argue that the lexical hierarchy should only include types which are not predictable; all other types should be implicitly introduced by a process of on-line type creation. This same on-line type construction also applies to new forms, giving them the same behavior as existing but predictable forms.

Consider a simple example. The type hierarchy in Figure 18 is a highly simplified analysis of the English past tense: words are cross-classified by lexeme and by inflectional class, and every word must be a

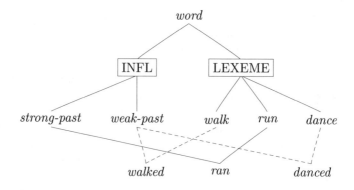

FIGURE 18 An underspecified type hierarchy

subtype of at least one maximal type in each of these two dimensions. The only maximal type that is not predictable is *ran*. Koenig and Jurafsky's proposal is that the other atomic types be left out of the hierarchy as it is specified. An on-line type construction procedure can build a 'virtual' type hierarchy that includes each possible subtype of one maximal subtype of *lexeme* and one maximal subtype of *infl*. This not only simplifies the type hierarchy, it also predicts that any new type added to the hierarchy will by default be a subtype of *weak-past*. The maximal subtypes of *strong-past* are all also subtypes of a particular lexeme, and so they will be incompatible with any new lexemes that come into the language. The only maximal subtype of *infl* that is sufficiently underspecified is *weak-past*, so new words will have no choice but to show weak past tense inflection.

3.4.3   Bringing it together

Using a combination of default inheritance and on-line type construction, we can now give a more complete presentation of the lexical organization described in §3.4.1. The relevant part of the lexical hierarchy is given in Figure 19.

As in §3.4.1, linking types specify the relationship between content and argument structure and realization types constrain the connection between argument structure and valence. For concreteness, assume the constraints in (73), based on Davis (1996), although the details will not be important.

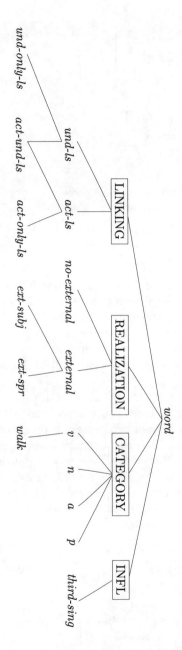

FIGURE 19 A hierarchy of word types

(73) a. *act-ls* →

$$
\begin{bmatrix}
\text{ARG-ST } \langle \text{NP:}\boxed{1},\ldots \rangle \\
\text{CONT} \quad \begin{bmatrix} \textit{act-rel} \\ \text{ACT } \boxed{1} \end{bmatrix}
\end{bmatrix}
$$

b. *und-ls* →

$$
\begin{bmatrix}
\text{ARG-ST } \langle \ldots, \text{NP:}\boxed{2},\ldots \rangle \\
\text{CONT} \quad \begin{bmatrix} \textit{und-rel} \\ \text{UND } \boxed{2} \end{bmatrix}
\end{bmatrix}
$$

c. *act-only-ls* →

$$
\begin{bmatrix}
\text{ARG-ST } \langle \text{NP} \rangle \\
\text{CONT} \quad \textit{act-only-rel}
\end{bmatrix}
$$

d. *und-only-ls* →

$$
\begin{bmatrix}
\text{ARG-ST } \langle \text{NP} \rangle \\
\text{CONT} \quad \textit{und-only-rel}
\end{bmatrix}
$$

The constraint in (73a) identifies the semantics of the actor role in a word's CONTENT with its first argument, and (73b) identifies the undergoer role with some argument position. So, if a verb has both an actor and an undergoer, the actor will be the first argument and the undergoer will be the second. If a verb has either an actor or an undergoer, but not both, then that single participant will be identified with the first argument position.

Realization types map argument structure to valence. Again, the detailed formalization of these constraints is not vital to my argument, but to be specific I will assume constraints along the lines of those proposed by Bouma et al. (in press). Function words, like determiners and coordinating conjunctions, don't have any argument structure and so the realization is trivial. Substantive words make a distinction between internal and external arguments. Internal (i.e., non-initial) arguments are always mapped to the COMPS list, at least in languages with nominative/accusative case marking.

(74) a. *no-external* →

$$
\begin{bmatrix} \text{HEAD } \textit{func} \end{bmatrix}
$$

b. *external* →

$$
\begin{bmatrix}
\text{HEAD} & \textit{subst} \\
\text{VAL} \,|\, \text{COMPS} & \boxed{1} - \textit{list(gap)} \\
\text{ARG-ST} & \langle \textit{synsem} \rangle \oplus \boxed{1}
\end{bmatrix}
$$

The non-initial arguments of a substantive word are either realized as complements or are of type *gap* and are realized via a long-distance dependency construction.

Substantives can be further divided according to how their external argument is realized:

(75) a. *ext-subj* →

$$\begin{bmatrix} \text{HEAD} & relational \\ \text{VAL|SUBJ} & \boxed{2} \\ \text{ARG-ST} & \langle \boxed{2}, \dots \rangle \end{bmatrix}$$

b. *ext-spr* →

$$\begin{bmatrix} \text{HEAD} & noun \\ \text{VAL|SPR} & \boxed{2} \\ \text{ARG-ST} & \langle \boxed{2}, \dots \rangle \end{bmatrix}$$

Relational words (e.g., verbs, prepositions, adjectives) realize their external argument as a subject, while nouns realize their external argument as a specifier.

The hierarchy in Figure 19 adds a fourth dimension the classification in §3.4.1, namely inflectional class. Inflectional classes determine the phonological form of a word. For example, there would be an inflectional class for regular third person singular verbs:

(76) *third-sg* →

$$\begin{bmatrix} \text{MORPH} & \begin{bmatrix} \text{ROOT} & \boxed{1} \\ \text{I-FORM} & f_{3sg}(\boxed{1}) \end{bmatrix} \\ \text{HEAD} & \begin{bmatrix} verb \\ \text{AGR } 3sg \end{bmatrix} \end{bmatrix}$$

The original gerund formation lexical rule can now be recast as an inflectional class:

(77) *vger* →

$$\begin{bmatrix} \text{MORPH} & \begin{bmatrix} \text{ROOT} & \boxed{1} \\ \text{I-FORM} & f_{ing}(\boxed{1}) \end{bmatrix} \\ \text{HEAD} & gerund \end{bmatrix}$$

This class, which is stipulated as being a subtype of *v*, overwrites the head value it inherits from that type.

The last dimension is category. The relevant constraints on category types were given in (72). Individual lexemes need only specify nonpredictable information. At a minimum, this will include a phonological form and a semantic relation:

(78) a. *walk* →

$$\begin{bmatrix} \text{MORPH} \,|\, \text{ROOT} & \langle walk \rangle \\ \text{CONT} & walk\text{-}rel \end{bmatrix}$$

Assume that the semantic type *walk-rel* is a subtype of *act-only-rel*.

Given these constraints, we can now apply on-line type construction to yield a virtual type hierarchy. The resulting hierarchy is given in Figure 20.[9] Each word inherits from at least one of the maximal types in each of the four dimensions: any word which satisfies this requirement is predicted to be a valid word.

Furthermore, the words in Figure 20 are the *only* words that will be generated. All other combinations of types will be ruled out by conflicting constraints. Demonstrating why this is so is somewhat tedious, but probably worth the effort.[10] The full yield of the hierarchy in Figure 19 is given in (79). Constraints that are in conflict are shaded.

(79) a. *third-sing & ext-subj & und-only-ls & walk* →

$$\begin{bmatrix} \text{MORPH} & \begin{bmatrix} \text{ROOT} & \boxed{1} \\ \text{I-FORM} & f_{3sg}(\boxed{1}) \end{bmatrix} \\ \text{HEAD} & \begin{bmatrix} relational \,/\, verb \\ \text{AGR } 3sg \end{bmatrix} \\ \text{VAL} \,|\, \text{SUBJ} & \boxed{2} \\ \text{ARG-ST} & \langle \boxed{2}\text{NP:}\boxed{3} \rangle \\ \text{CONT} & \begin{bmatrix} \boxed{walk\text{-}rel \;\&\; und\text{-}only\text{-}rel} \\ \text{ACT } \boxed{3} \end{bmatrix} \end{bmatrix}$$

---

[9] Note that this hierarchy is orthogonal to the one in (98) on page 65. The hierarchy in Figure 20 is a classification of *signs*, while the hierarchy in (98) is a classification of *head* objects (see §1.4.2).

[10] In fact, in producing (79) I discovered that many of the cases were not in fact ruled out by anything unless I added the strengthened constraints in (72).

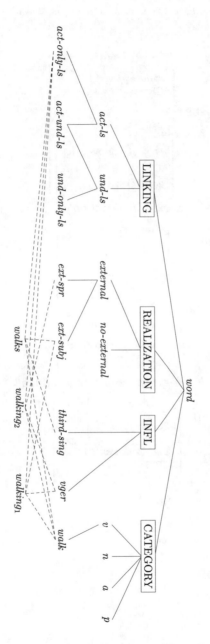

FIGURE 20 A completed type hierarchy

b. *third-sing & ext-subj & act-und-ls & walk* →

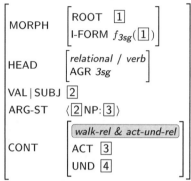

$$
\begin{bmatrix}
\text{MORPH} & \begin{bmatrix} \text{ROOT} & \boxed{1} \\ \text{I-FORM} & f_{3sg}(\boxed{1}) \end{bmatrix} \\[1em]
\text{HEAD} & \begin{bmatrix} relational \;/\; verb \\ \text{AGR } 3sg \end{bmatrix} \\[1em]
\text{VAL}\,|\,\text{SUBJ} & \boxed{2} \\
\text{ARG-ST} & \langle \boxed{2}\,\text{NP:}\boxed{3} \rangle \\[0.5em]
\text{CONT} & \begin{bmatrix} \boxed{walk\text{-}rel \;\&\; act\text{-}und\text{-}rel} \\ \text{ACT } \boxed{3} \\ \text{UND } \boxed{4} \end{bmatrix}
\end{bmatrix}
$$

c. *third-sing & ext-subj & act-only-ls & walk* →

$$
\begin{bmatrix}
\text{MORPH} & \begin{bmatrix} \text{ROOT} & \boxed{1} \\ \text{I-FORM} & f_{3sg}(\boxed{1}) \end{bmatrix} \\[1em]
\text{HEAD} & \begin{bmatrix} relational \;/\; verb \\ \text{AGR } 3sg \end{bmatrix} \\[1em]
\text{VAL}\,|\,\text{SUBJ} & \boxed{2} \\
\text{ARG-ST} & \langle \boxed{2}\,\text{NP:}\boxed{3} \rangle \\[0.5em]
\text{CONT} & \begin{bmatrix} walk\text{-}rel \;\&\; act\text{-}only\text{-}rel \\ \text{ACT } \boxed{3} \end{bmatrix}
\end{bmatrix}
$$

d. *third-sing & ext-spr & und-only-ls & walk* →

$$
\begin{bmatrix}
\text{MORPH} & \begin{bmatrix} \text{ROOT} & \boxed{1} \\ \text{I-FORM} & f_{3sg}(\boxed{1}) \end{bmatrix} \\[1em]
\text{HEAD} & \begin{bmatrix} \boxed{noun \;\&\; relational} \\ \text{AGR } 3sg \end{bmatrix} \\[1em]
\text{VAL}\,|\,\text{SPR} & \boxed{2} \\
\text{ARG-ST} & \langle \boxed{2}\,\text{NP:}\boxed{3} \rangle \\[0.5em]
\text{CONT} & \begin{bmatrix} \boxed{walk\text{-}rel \;\&\; und\text{-}only\text{-}rel} \\ \text{UND } \boxed{4} \end{bmatrix}
\end{bmatrix}
$$

e. *third-sing & ext-spr & act-und-ls & walk* →

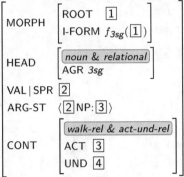

$$
\begin{bmatrix}
\text{MORPH} & \begin{bmatrix} \text{ROOT} & \boxed{1} \\ \text{I-FORM} & f_{3sg}(\boxed{1}) \end{bmatrix} \\[2ex]
\text{HEAD} & \begin{bmatrix} \boxed{noun\ \&\ relational} \\ \text{AGR } 3sg \end{bmatrix} \\[2ex]
\text{VAL} \mid \text{SPR} & \boxed{2} \\
\text{ARG-ST} & \langle \boxed{2}\text{NP:}\boxed{3} \rangle \\[1ex]
\text{CONT} & \begin{bmatrix} \boxed{walk\text{-}rel\ \&\ act\text{-}und\text{-}rel} \\ \text{ACT } \boxed{3} \\ \text{UND } \boxed{4} \end{bmatrix}
\end{bmatrix}
$$

f. *third-sing & ext-spr & act-only-ls & walk* →

$$
\begin{bmatrix}
\text{MORPH} & \begin{bmatrix} \text{ROOT} & \boxed{1} \\ \text{I-FORM} & f_{3sg}(\boxed{1}) \end{bmatrix} \\[2ex]
\text{HEAD} & \begin{bmatrix} \boxed{noun\ \&\ relational} \\ \text{AGR } 3sg \end{bmatrix} \\[2ex]
\text{VAL} \mid \text{SPR} & \boxed{2} \\
\text{ARG-ST} & \langle \boxed{2}\text{NP:}\boxed{3} \rangle \\[1ex]
\text{CONT} & \begin{bmatrix} walk\text{-}rel\ \&\ act\text{-}only\text{-}rel \\ \text{ACT } \boxed{3} \end{bmatrix}
\end{bmatrix}
$$

g. *third-sing & no-ext & und-only-ls & walk* →

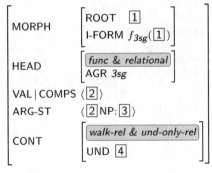

$$
\begin{bmatrix}
\text{MORPH} & \begin{bmatrix} \text{ROOT} & \boxed{1} \\ \text{I-FORM} & f_{3sg}(\boxed{1}) \end{bmatrix} \\[2ex]
\text{HEAD} & \begin{bmatrix} \boxed{func\ \&\ relational} \\ \text{AGR } 3sg \end{bmatrix} \\[2ex]
\text{VAL} \mid \text{COMPS} & \langle \boxed{2} \rangle \\
\text{ARG-ST} & \langle \boxed{2}\text{NP:}\boxed{3} \rangle \\[1ex]
\text{CONT} & \begin{bmatrix} \boxed{walk\text{-}rel\ \&\ und\text{-}only\text{-}rel} \\ \text{UND } \boxed{4} \end{bmatrix}
\end{bmatrix}
$$

h. *third-sing & no-ext & act-und-ls & walk* →

$$
\begin{bmatrix}
\text{MORPH} & \begin{bmatrix} \text{ROOT} & \boxed{1} \\ \text{I-FORM } f_{3sg}(\boxed{1}) \end{bmatrix} \\[2ex]
\text{HEAD} & \begin{bmatrix} \boxed{\textit{func \& relational}} \\ \text{AGR } 3sg \end{bmatrix} \\[2ex]
\text{VAL | COMPS} & \langle \boxed{2} \rangle \\
\text{ARG-ST} & \langle \boxed{2}\text{NP:}\boxed{3} \rangle \\[1ex]
\text{CONT} & \begin{bmatrix} \boxed{\textit{walk-rel \& act-und-rel}} \\ \text{ACT } \boxed{3} \\ \text{UND } \boxed{4} \end{bmatrix}
\end{bmatrix}
$$

i. *third-sing & no-ext & act-only-ls & walk* →

$$
\begin{bmatrix}
\text{MORPH} & \begin{bmatrix} \text{ROOT} & \boxed{1} \\ \text{I-FORM } f_{3sg}(\boxed{1}) \end{bmatrix} \\[2ex]
\text{HEAD} & \begin{bmatrix} \boxed{\textit{func \& relational}} \\ \text{AGR } 3sg \end{bmatrix} \\[2ex]
\text{VAL | COMPS} & \langle \boxed{2} \rangle \\
\text{ARG-ST} & \langle \boxed{2}\text{NP:}\boxed{3} \rangle \\[1ex]
\text{CONT} & \begin{bmatrix} \textit{walk-rel \& act-only-rel} \\ \text{ACT } \boxed{3} \end{bmatrix}
\end{bmatrix}
$$

j. *vger & ext-subj & und-only-ls & walk* →

$$
\begin{bmatrix}
\text{MORPH} & \begin{bmatrix} \text{ROOT} & \boxed{1} \\ \text{I-FORM } f_{ing}(\boxed{1}) \end{bmatrix} \\[2ex]
\text{HEAD} & \begin{bmatrix} \textit{gerund} \\ \text{AGR } 3sg \end{bmatrix} \\[2ex]
\text{VAL | SUBJ} & \boxed{2} \\
\text{ARG-ST} & \langle \boxed{2}\text{NP:}\boxed{3} \rangle \\[1ex]
\text{CONT} & \begin{bmatrix} \boxed{\textit{walk-rel \& und-only-rel}} \\ \text{ACT } \boxed{3} \end{bmatrix}
\end{bmatrix}
$$

k. *vger & ext-subj & act-und-ls & walk* →

$$
\begin{bmatrix}
\text{MORPH} & \begin{bmatrix} \text{ROOT} & \boxed{1} \\ \text{I-FORM } f_{ing}(\boxed{1}) \end{bmatrix} \\[2ex]
\text{HEAD} & \begin{bmatrix} gerund \\ \text{AGR } 3sg \end{bmatrix} \\[2ex]
\text{VAL | SUBJ} & \boxed{2} \\
\text{ARG-ST} & \langle \boxed{2}\,\text{NP:}\boxed{3} \rangle \\[2ex]
\text{CONT} & \begin{bmatrix} \boxed{walk\text{-}rel \ \& \ act\text{-}und\text{-}rel} \\ \text{ACT } \boxed{3} \\ \text{UND } \boxed{4} \end{bmatrix}
\end{bmatrix}
$$

l. *vger & ext-subj & act-only-ls & walk* →

$$
\begin{bmatrix}
\text{MORPH} & \begin{bmatrix} \text{ROOT} & \boxed{1} \\ \text{I-FORM } f_{ing}(\boxed{1}) \end{bmatrix} \\[2ex]
\text{HEAD} & \begin{bmatrix} gerund \\ \text{AGR } 3sg \end{bmatrix} \\[2ex]
\text{VAL | SUBJ} & \boxed{2} \\
\text{ARG-ST} & \langle \boxed{2}\,\text{NP:}\boxed{3} \rangle \\[2ex]
\text{CONT} & \begin{bmatrix} walk\text{-}rel \ \& \ act\text{-}only\text{-}rel \\ \text{ACT } \boxed{3} \end{bmatrix}
\end{bmatrix}
$$

m. *vger & ext-spr & und-only-ls & walk* →

$$
\begin{bmatrix}
\text{MORPH} & \begin{bmatrix} \text{ROOT} & \boxed{1} \\ \text{I-FORM } f_{ing}(\boxed{1}) \end{bmatrix} \\[2ex]
\text{HEAD} & \begin{bmatrix} gerund \\ \text{AGR } 3sg \end{bmatrix} \\[2ex]
\text{VAL | SPR} & \boxed{2} \\
\text{ARG-ST} & \langle \boxed{2}\,\text{NP:}\boxed{3} \rangle \\[2ex]
\text{CONT} & \begin{bmatrix} \boxed{walk\text{-}rel \ \& \ und\text{-}only\text{-}rel} \\ \text{UND } \boxed{4} \end{bmatrix}
\end{bmatrix}
$$

n. *vger & ext-spr & act-und-ls & walk* →

$$
\begin{bmatrix}
\text{MORPH} & \begin{bmatrix} \text{ROOT} & \boxed{1} \\ \text{I-FORM } f_{ing}(\boxed{1}) \end{bmatrix} \\[2ex]
\text{HEAD} & \begin{bmatrix} gerund \\ \text{AGR } 3sg \end{bmatrix} \\[2ex]
\text{VAL | SPR} & \boxed{2} \\
\text{ARG-ST} & \langle \boxed{2}\text{NP:}\boxed{3} \rangle \\[1ex]
\text{CONT} & \begin{bmatrix} \boxed{walk\text{-}rel\ \&\ act\text{-}und\text{-}rel} \\ \text{ACT } \boxed{3} \\ \text{UND } \boxed{4} \end{bmatrix}
\end{bmatrix}
$$

o. *vger & ext-spr & act-only-ls & walk* →

$$
\begin{bmatrix}
\text{MORPH} & \begin{bmatrix} \text{ROOT} & \boxed{1} \\ \text{I-FORM } f_{ing}(\boxed{1}) \end{bmatrix} \\[2ex]
\text{HEAD} & \begin{bmatrix} gerund \\ \text{AGR } 3sg \end{bmatrix} \\[2ex]
\text{VAL | SPR} & \boxed{2} \\
\text{ARG-ST} & \langle \boxed{2}\text{NP:}\boxed{3} \rangle \\[1ex]
\text{CONT} & \begin{bmatrix} walk\text{-}rel\ \&\ act\text{-}only\text{-}rel \\ \text{ACT } \boxed{3} \end{bmatrix}
\end{bmatrix}
$$

p. *vger & no-ext & und-only-ls & walk* →

$$
\begin{bmatrix}
\text{MORPH} & \begin{bmatrix} \text{ROOT} & \boxed{1} \\ \text{I-FORM } f_{ing}(\boxed{1}) \end{bmatrix} \\[2ex]
\text{HEAD} & \begin{bmatrix} \boxed{gerund\ \&\ func} \\ \text{AGR } 3sg \end{bmatrix} \\[2ex]
\text{VAL | COMPS} & \langle \boxed{2} \rangle \\
\text{ARG-ST} & \langle \boxed{2}\text{NP:}\boxed{3} \rangle \\[1ex]
\text{CONT} & \begin{bmatrix} \boxed{walk\text{-}rel\ \&\ und\text{-}only\text{-}rel} \\ \text{UND } \boxed{4} \end{bmatrix}
\end{bmatrix}
$$

q. *vger & no-ext & act-und-ls & walk* →

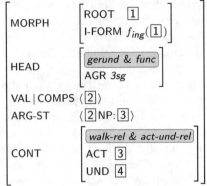

r. *vger & no-ext & act-only-ls & walk* →

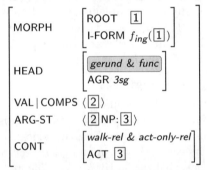

The only combinations of types that do not have conflicting constraints on them are given in (79c), (79l), and (79o). These three types correspond to the third person singular form, the ACC-*ing* gerund, and the POSS-*ing* gerund, respectively.

The effect of the type *vger* is the same as that of the Gerund Formation Lexical Rule. Since *gerund* is a subtype of *noun* in the hierarchy in (69), a phrase projected by a gerund will be able to occur anywhere an NP is selected for. Thus, verbal gerund phrases will have the external distribution of NPs. Adverbs modify objects of category *relational*, which include verbs, adjectives, and verbal gerunds, among other things. Since adjectives only modify *c(ommon)-nouns*, verbal gerund phrases will contain adverbial rather than adjectival modifiers. Since *verb* is a distinct subclass of *relational* disjoint from *gerund*, verbal gerund phrases will not have the distribution of true VPs.

Because a gerund has a *psoa* content just like a verb does, its semantic roles will get linked to argument positions just like a verb's do. *Gerund* is a subtype of *subst*, so its non-initial arguments will get mapped to the COMPS list, and a gerund will take the same complements as the verb from which it is derived. But, *gerund* is a subtype of both *noun* and *relational*, so a gerund's external argument could get mapped either to the subject or to the specifier. Thus we get the effect of the old gerund lexical rule, without having to stipulate the exceptional argument mapping.

This kind of analysis is much more restrictive than the lexical rule analysis. One could write a lexical rule that produces a gerund which takes a subject like a verb does but cannot take complements, even though cross-linguistically gerunds of that type do not seem to occur. Under the approach sketched here, the only way for a word to take a subject is for it to be a subtype of *ext-subj*. Since *ext-subj* is a subtype of *external*, anything that is a subtype of *ext-subj* will also inherit all of the constraints associated with *external*. In other words, anything that takes a subject will potentially take complements too. Similarly, VFORM values are only appropriate for objects of type *verb*. That means that any gerund that inflects like a finite verb (and thus is [VFORM fin]) will also by necessity inherit from *ext-subj*.

3.4.4 Gerunds in ergative languages

So far, the primary objection to the Gerund Formation Lexical Rule that I have offered is that it fails to sufficiently constrain the possible range of variation. The previous section showed how the lexical rule could be eliminated in favor of an inflectional type in an underspecified type hierarchy to account for the Deverbalization Hierarchy. The underlying idea is the same for both approaches. Only the implementation is different.

However, the astute reader will have noticed that the lexical rule and the underspecified type hierarchy just outlined actually make different predictions for some languages. The lexical rule is an operation that manipulates valence structure. For a POSS-*ing* gerund, it takes the subject of the underlying verb and makes it the specifier of the gerund. The type hierarchy approach on the other hand works at the level of argument structure. The first argument of the underlying verb, which would have been realized as its subject, is instead realized as the specifier of the gerund.

In a language like English, the unmarked realization for the first argument is always as the grammatical subject. Manning (1996) argues that ergative languages differ from accusative languages in that the subject is not always the highest argument. For an intransitive verb, the single core argument is realized as the subject, but for a transitive verb the second argument is the subject:

(80)

	INTRANSITIVE	TRANSITIVE
ACCUSATIVE	$\begin{bmatrix} \text{SUBJ} & \langle \boxed{1}\text{NP}[nom]\rangle \\ \text{COMPS} & \langle\ \rangle \\ \text{ARG-ST} & \langle \boxed{1}\rangle \end{bmatrix}$	$\begin{bmatrix} \text{SUBJ} & \langle \boxed{1}\text{NP}[nom]\rangle \\ \text{COMPS} & \langle \boxed{2}\text{NP}[acc]\rangle \\ \text{ARG-ST} & \langle \boxed{1}, \boxed{2}\rangle \end{bmatrix}$
ERGATIVE	$\begin{bmatrix} \text{SUBJ} & \langle \boxed{1}\text{NP}[abs]\rangle \\ \text{COMPS} & \langle\ \rangle \\ \text{ARG-ST} & \langle \boxed{1}\rangle \end{bmatrix}$	$\begin{bmatrix} \text{SUBJ} & \langle \boxed{2}\text{NP}[abs]\rangle \\ \text{COMPS} & \langle \boxed{1}\text{NP}[erg]\rangle \\ \text{ARG-ST} & \langle \boxed{1}, \boxed{2}\rangle \end{bmatrix}$

Given this view of ergativity, the Gerund Formation Lexical Rule predicts that in an ergative language a gerund formed from a transitive verb should take the verb's absolutive argument as a specifier. The hierarchical approach in contrast predicts that such a gerund should take the verb's ergative argument as a specifier.

In at least one ergative language, Jacaltec, the second prediction is borne out. Jacaltec is a head-marking language, so case relations are indicated via person and number agreement on the verb:

(81) a. X-Ø-to-pax   heb naj winaj
          PST-3ABS-go-back PL   the man
          'The men returned.'   (Foley and Van Valin 1984, 279)

   b. X-Ø-aw-il   ix
       PST-3ABS-2SG.ERG-see she
       'You saw her.'

In addition to indicating the highest ranking argument of a transitive verb, ergative case is also used to mark possession within noun phrases:

(82) hin-xañab
      1SG.GEN-sandal
      'my sandals'   (Foley and Van Valin 1984, 279)

To avoid confusion, I will gloss this use of ergative case as 'genitive,' even though it is formally identical to the ergative case used in transitive clauses.

Jacaltec has a construction comparable to the English POSS-*ing* verbal gerund in which a verb and its arguments acts as an argument of a higher verb. If the verb is intransitive, its sole argument takes genitive case:

(83) a. Ch-Ø-aw-iche   ha-munlayi
          NPST-3ABS-2SG.ERG-begin 2SG.GEN-work
          'You begin to work.' (lit: 'You begin it – you work.')
                          (Foley and Van Valin 1984, 290)

   b. Ch-∅-ichi   ha-munlayi
      NPST-3ABS-begin 2SG.GEN-work
      'You begin to work.' (lit: 'It begins – you work.')

The question to ask now is, which argument of a transitive verb gets genitive case in this construction? The answer is that the ergative argument does:

(84) a. X-∅-(y)-il   ix hin-ha-mak-ni
       PST-3ABS-3ERG-see she 1SG.ABS-2SG.GEN-hit-NOM
       'She saw you hit me.'   (Foley and Van Valin 1984, 289)
    b. X-∅-w-ilwe   ∅-hin-watx'e-n   kap
       PST-3ABS-1SG.ERG-try 3ABS-1SG.GEN-make-NOM the
       camïxe (an)
       shirt   me
       'I tried to make the shirt.'

This pattern is inconsistent with the Gerund Formation Lexical Rule, since it is not the subject of a transitive verb that appears as a possessor in this construction. However, this is exactly what we would expect if gerunds are actually verbs whose arguments are realized following the nominal realization patterns. NPs in Jacaltec, as in many other syntactically ergative languages (Silverstein 1993), follow a nominative/accusative case marking pattern. So, the highest argument of the verb is realized as a possessor regardless of the grammatical relation it normally would receive. Thus Jacaltec gerunds provide further support for deriving the effect of gerund formation through the interaction of constraints in the lexical hierarchy rather than by a lexical rule.

3.4.5 Explaining the LCH

The implicational structure of the Deverbalization Hierarchy is directly reflected by the subsumption ordering in the lexical hierarchy in Figure 20. In a weak sense of the word, this explains the behavior of the English verbal gerund. The properties of the English verbal gerund follow from the structure of the English lexical hierarchy, which in turn is motivated independently by other lexical constructions in English.

The Deverbalization Hierarchy however is a universal claim about gerunds in all languages. It would be absurd to try to explain a universal pattern in terms of parochial facts about the structure of the English lexicon. If the lexical patterns in Figure 20 are to serve as an explanation for a universal property of language, they themselves must be universal. Obviously, the specific details of Figure 20 cannot be universal. At best only the general outlines of the organization of the lexicon could be universal, and even then there is considerable variation. For example, as we saw in §3.4.4, Manning (1996) shows that nominative/accusative and ergative/absolutive languages have very different realization constraints, and Manning and Sag (1999) analyze a number of diathesis alternations as alternative realizations of a basic argument structure.

The best we can say is that there seem to be very general principles that govern the structure of the lexicon of all languages. A good candidate for such a principle is that the mapping of semantic roles to syntactic positions is mediated by a level of syntacticized argument structure. This entails that the lexical hierarchy of every language will be divided into at least the three dimensions discussed above in §3.4.1. Within each dimension, a language can avail itself of a limited number of choices out of a universal inventory of organizational schemes (say, nominative vs. ergative case marking).[11] Then, with those choices, come a set of unmarked type constraints that a language is likely to incorporate into its grammar. That is, the particular type constraints offered in the previous section are good candidates for universal archetypes, in the sense of §1.5. So, while the particular type hierarchy in Figure 20 is particular to English, its general organization and many of the types in it are cross-linguistically unmarked, and therefore we should not be surprised to find similar lexical hierarchies in grammars of language after language.

---

[11]See §1.5 and §4.2.1 for a discussion of where such a universal inventory might come from.

4

Conclusions and Consequences

4.1 A look back

As we saw in the first chapter, grammatical categories are central to generative theories of grammar. It is typically assumed that there is a small number of primitive, probably universal, probably innate grammatical categories. However, this view of parts of speech is in large part a legacy of traditional grammar, and several alternatives to the traditional system of parts of speech have been proposed. One notable example is McCawley (1982), who argues for an approach that "...avoids the notion of syntactic category as such, operating instead directly in terms of a number of distinct factors to which syntactic phenomena can be sensitive; in this view, syntactic category names will merely be informal abbreviations for combinations of these factors" (185). A similar approach to categories was taken by Pollard and Sag (1987), who observe that "equipped with the notions of head features and subcategorization, we are now in a position to *define* conventional grammatical symbols such as NP, VP, etc. in terms of feature structures of type sign" (68).

Taking this approach to syntactic categories as a foundation, I have presented here an analysis of mixed category constructions, which pose a serious problem for the traditional view of syntactic categories. One kind of mixed category construction, the English verbal gerund (e.g., *Kim's watching television* or *Chris giving Pat the book*), much like similar constructions in Korean, Turkish, Fijian, Quechua, and many other languages, seem to be neither nouns nor verbs but a mix of both. Specifically, as we saw in §2.1, verbal gerund phrases have four basic properties that need to be accounted for: (i) the gerund plus its complements have the internal distribution of a VP; (ii) verbal gerunds are modified by adverbs, not adjectives; (iii) the optional subject of the gerund can be either a genitive or an accusative NP; and (iv) the entire gerund phrase has the external distribution of an NP. This mix of nominal and verbal properties provides a challenge to any syntactic framework that assumes a strict version of X-bar theory.

Various approaches have been proposed in the literature to get around these problems. While these analyses differ greatly in their technical details, as discussed in §2.2 they all assign verbal gerund phrases some variation of the following structure:

(1)

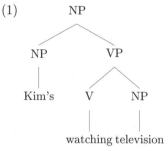

This reflects the traditional description of verbal gerund phrases as 'verbal inside, nominal outside' quite literally by giving verbal gerund phrases a V node dominated by an NP node. However, in order to license a structure like (1), each of these analyses requires abandoning a fundamentally desirable theoretical assumption or adopting a highly abstract structure for which independent motivation is difficult to find.

An ideal analysis of verbal gerunds in English would be able to account for their mixed verbal/nominal properties without the addition of otherwise unmotivated mechanisms. Section 2.3 showed how the properties of verbal gerunds can be accounted for by the Gerund Formation Lexical Rule, which expresses the regular relation between the present participle form of a verb and its gerund form:

$$
(2) \quad
\begin{bmatrix}
\text{HEAD} & \begin{bmatrix} \textit{verb} \\ \text{VFORM } \textit{prp} \end{bmatrix} \\
\text{VALENCE} & \begin{bmatrix} \text{SUBJ} & \langle \boxed{1}\text{NP} \rangle \\ \text{COMPS} & \boxed{2} \\ \text{SPR} & \langle \, \rangle \end{bmatrix}
\end{bmatrix}
\implies
\begin{bmatrix}
\text{HEAD} & \textit{gerund} \\
\text{VALENCE} & \begin{bmatrix} \text{SUBJ} & \langle \boxed{1} \rangle \\ \text{COMPS} & \boxed{2} \\ \text{SPR} & \langle \boxed{1} \rangle \end{bmatrix}
\end{bmatrix}
$$

The distribution of verbal gerund phrases then can be accounted for by the (partial) hierarchy of HEAD values in (98), repeated here as (3).

(3)

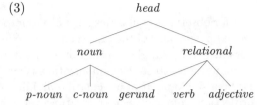

Since *gerund* is a subtype of *noun,* a phrase projected by a gerund
will be able to occur anywhere an NP is selected for. Thus, verbal
gerunds will have the external distribution of NPs. Adverbs modify objects of category *relational,* which include verbs, adjectives, and verbal
gerunds, among other things. Since adjectives only modify *c(ommon)-
nouns,* verbal gerunds will contain adverbial rather than adjectival modifiers. Since *verb* is a distinct subclass of *relational* disjoint from *gerund,*
verbal gerunds will not have the distribution of true VPs. This cross-
classification directly reflects the traditional view of gerunds as intermediate between nouns and verbs. However, by formalizing this intuitive
view as a cross-classification of HEAD values, we can localize the idiosyncratic behavior of verbal gerunds to the lexicon.

Finally, since a gerund selects for both a subject and a specifier, it
will be eligible to head either a *nonfin-head-subj-cx,* which combines a
head with an accusative NP subject, or a *noun-poss-cx,* which combines
a head with a genitive NP specifier. The differences in the distribution of
verbal gerunds with accusative subjects and genitive specifiers that are
found with respect to agreement, pied piping, and quantifier scope follow
from the differences between the two constructions. The *nonfin-head-
subj-cx* construction is a type of clause and so accusative subject verbal
gerund phrases inherit many of the properties of non-finite clauses. Since
genitive subject gerunds are instances of the *noun-poss-cx* construction,
they inherit many of the properties of noun phrases.

Thus, by exploiting HPSG's hierarchical classification of category
types and its inventory of elaborated phrase structure rules, we are able
to account for the mixed behavior of verbal gerunds without adding any
additional theoretical mechanisms or weakening any basic assumptions.

This analysis of English gerunds can account for their properties by
situating them within a more fine-grained theory of syntactic categories.
What remains to be explained then is why certain sets of word classes
have significant overlap while others are disjoint, and why the same sets
of overlapping word classes tend to be found in language after language.
It may be true that in principle dimensions like lexical category, semantic
type, and valence can vary independently, it remains a fact that 'normal'
nouns do not take accusative subjects or objects, and 'normal' verbs do

not take genitive specifiers.

One approach to account for observed regularities has been to impose a structural condition on mixed projections of the type seen in (1). Since, in English at least, specifiers attach to a higher projection that complements, one could rule out many non-attested nominalization types by stipulating that there must be a single point of articulation dividing the nominal part of a mixed projection from the verbal part. However, when we looked in detail at the cross-linguistic variation in §3.3, we saw that this structural condition is unable to straightforwardly account for the data. Instead, what is needed is a condition on lexical entries that limits what kinds of mixed lexical properties can occur.

Along side the strictly extensional, discrete view of categories of generative grammar, more radical alternative have also been developed. Researchers in functional and cognitive approaches to language have proposed theories of prototype categories (Lakoff 1987, Langacker 1987a, Croft 1991). In sharp contrast to formal grammar's innate parts of speech, prototype categories allow gradient membership and perhaps reflect general cognitive organization in a more natural way (e.g. Rosch 1978). However, allowing partial category membership undermines the algebraic foundation of formal grammar (Taylor 1995), and it has been difficult to reconcile the results of the two approaches.

Section 3.4 showed how default inheritance type hierarchies provide one way to combine formal and functional approaches in a way that benefits from the best of both. Prototype categories are represented as default constraints on types high up in the type hierarchy. Since such types tend to be very general and to have many subtypes, the properties of the prototype will be inherited by the 'regular' maximal types. But, since the prototype is expressed as a default, subtypes of it can impose more specific constraints that override the constraints associated with the prototype. Thus we can account for both the regularities found across instances of a grammatical category and we can account for the systematic irregularities found in mixed categories.

4.2 A look forward

The preceeding chapters have presented novel analyses of several constructions which have proven vexing over the years. However, the general techniques developed have consequences that extend well beyond those constructions.

4.2.1 Universals in HPSG

The explanation for the Deverbalization Hierarchy that was ultimately proposed in §3.4 was that part of the lexical hierarchy of every language is drawn from an inventory of universally available archetypes. There are at least two ways of thinking about this kind of model of language universals.

Current work on language universals generally falls into one of two camps, the generative approach and the typological approach (Comrie 1989, Greenberg 1990). One difference between the two approaches to universals is that in the typological model, linguistic universals are generalizations about possible *languages,* while in the generative model, universals are generalizations about possible *grammars*: "The study of linguistic universals is the study of the properties of any generative grammar for a natural language" (Chomsky 1965, 28). This is not a trivial difference. As Greenberg (1990) observes, the focus on synchronic grammars to the exclusion of, say, usage frequency or historical change, sharply restricts both "the range of relevant data to be explained and the nature of the explanations themselves" (710).

Following the generative tradition, we could assume that archetypes are universally available either due to more general properties of human cognition or perhaps simply because they are innate. Other parts of the lexical hierarchy are then chosen from a set of universally available types. These in a sense come 'for free', since their existence is entailed by something about the way language works, and they provide the cross-linguistic motivation for the language specific types that inherit from them. Finally, the lower reaches of the lexical hierarchy are populated by strictly parochial types that have no cross-linguistic generality and reflect the uniqueness of each human language.

Alternatively, we could suppose that the lexical hierarchy of each language, and indeed for each speaker of each language, is unique, built up perhaps along the lines discussed by Green (1997). Similarities between grammars of different languages arise from the similar diachronic and functional pressures that shape each language. This is the kind of model that Croft (1995, 504) calls typological functionalism:

> Some typologists have argued for grammatical analyses that integrate form and function more profoundly than other mixed models. These accept that the grammar includes arbitrariness, and they provide mixed analyses. However, the mixed analyses are such that the arbitrary parts of the analysis are language-specific, while the universal properties instantiated in the analysis are functional.

Typological functionalism makes an attractive way of integrating formal and functional approaches to language without substantially weakening either. It would allow a formal grammarian to draw on, for example, the competition models proposed by Bates and MacWhinney (1989) or DuBois (1985) without necessarily abandoning the idea that grammar is an arbitrary, self-contained, symbolic system.

Finally, it is important to note that these two views of universals are not mutually exclusive. The kinds of functional analysis appealed to by typological functionalists tend to be stated in a relatively imprecise manner that makes the exact predictions they make for synchronic grammars hard to evaluate. One might think of Ackerman and Webelhuth's (1998) universal archetypes as a particular solution to what Kirby (1997) calls the Problem of Linkage:

(4) THE PROBLEM OF LINKAGE
How does a universal property of language use give rise to a restriction on the distribution of occurring languages in the space of possible languages?

Even in a typological functionalist model of language, there must be some link between the universal properties of language and the parochial properties of individual languages. We can think of archetypes as a technical device for providing that link.

These are the philosophical positions one could take towards archetypes in general. What then about the particular archetypes I propose here? The key archetypes in (72) are repeated here:

(5) a. $v \rightarrow$
$$\begin{bmatrix} \text{HEAD } relational \ / \ verb \\ \text{CONT } psoa \end{bmatrix}$$

b. $n \rightarrow$
$$\begin{bmatrix} \text{HEAD } noun \ / \ c\text{-}noun \\ \text{CONT } nom\text{-}obj \end{bmatrix}$$

These constraints say that by default, nouns are words that denote objects and verbs are words that denote actions.

Now the questions is, what is the status of these constraints? Are they hard-wired as part of Universal Grammar, or are they derived from something outside of grammar? Unfortunately, this is not the sort of question that the present study is designed to answer. Looking at gerund constructions in a wide variety of languages will tell us which gerund types are widespread and which are unique to particular languages, but it seems unlikely that it will shed any light on the source of those properties.

However, there is some evidence from other work that suggests that the archetypes in (5) do indeed follow from something outside of grammar. In particular, the semantic bootstrapping hypothesis (Grimshaw

1981, Macnamara 1982, Pinker 1982, Pinker 1989) claims that children learning language use semantic types as a basis for syntactic classification. That is:

> ...certain cognitive categories have what I will call Canonical Structural Realization (CSR): CSR(object) = N, CSR(action) = V. [Language acquisition] employs a CSR principle: a word belongs to its CSR, unless there is evidence to the contrary (Grimshaw 1981, 174).

If we suppose, following Green (1997), that language acquisition is a process of incrementally building a type hierarchy, then Grimshaw's CSR principle will guarantee that types more or less like those in (5) will be introduced into the child's grammar early on, and will be high up in the adult hierarchy.

Thus, the constraints in (5) may be archetypes due to a heuristic employed by language learners and not due to anything fundamental about grammatical representation itself. Note that there is no contradiction in saying the constraints in (5) are archetypes and they can be derived from something outside the grammatical system. Archetypes as I use them here provide the link between language universals and grammatical particulars, but embody no specific claim as to the origin of those universals.

4.2.2 Lexical integrity

HPSG is a lexicalist framework, and as such it takes the Lexical Integrity Principle as an important organizing principle for linguistic knowledge. However, exactly what lexical integrity means given a model of grammar like the one used here is not entirely clear. In this section some of the issues surrounding lexical integrity raised by the analyses in the previous chapters will be discussed.

Intuitively, the Lexical Integrity Principle can be given a straightforward definition:

(6) LEXICAL INTEGRITY PRINCIPLE
The syntax neither manipulates nor has access to the internal form of words (Anderson 1992, 84).

Translating this into something that either constrains a grammatical theory or, better yet, can be derived from a grammatical theory is more difficult. Ackerman and Webelhuth (1998) argue that lexicalism is actually a cluster concept that can be broken down into at least three "lexicalist proto-principles" which a linguistic theory may adopt independently.

The first two proto-principles are morphological integrity and lexical adicity. Ackerman and Webelhuth define morphological integrity as the principle that syntactic mechanisms neither make reference to the daughters of morphological words nor can they create new morphological words in constituent structure. Simply put, this is the claim that words are syntactic atoms. This is a familiar aspect of lexical integrity. For example, rules of adjunction allow modifiers to be inserted in most kinds of syntactic phrases: *the cat* vs. *the big cat, walked slowly* vs. *walked very slowly, the cat walked* vs. *the cat usually walked.* But, modifiers cannot be inserted in morphologically constructed elements, even when the combination makes perfect sense semantically (*walk-slowly-ed, *slow-very-ly). The second proto-principle, lexical adicity, is somewhat more abstract. This is the principle that the adicity of a lexical item is lexically fully determined and cannot be altered by items of the syntactic context in which it appears. That is, valence changing operations, like passives and causatives, are essentially lexical in nature. The third proto-principle, morphological expression, is not relevant for this discussion.

The first of these principles, morphological integrity, follows from the model of the lexicon presented by Flickinger (1987) and Pollard and Sag (1987). The output of a lexical rule contains no information about the derivational history of the input, so it follows that that information will be unavailable to the syntax. Other versions of HPSG morphology (e.g., Riehemann 1998) do not have this property, and so morphological integrity must be stipulated as a meta-constraint on possible syntactic constraints.

In many frameworks, lexical adicity follows from the nature of the interface between the syntax and the lexicon. For example, for Anderson (1992, 92) it is a special case of a general Monotonicity Principle:

(7) The only effect a syntactic principle can have on a morphosyntactic representation is to add features to it.

Here 'morphosyntactic representation' has a specific technical meaning: it is the syntactically relevant part of the information associated with a lexical entry, and includes information about category and inflection, but not derivation.

In order to evaluate a principle like lexical adicity in any particular framework, one must know where the division between 'the lexicon' and 'the syntax' is drawn in that particular framework. Ackerman and Webelhuth claim that in HPSG lexical adicity does not follow from any more general principles. In fact, they argue, it is violated by so-called 'argument attraction' analyses (e.g., Hinrichs and Nakazawa 1989, 1990), in which a head combines with an unsaturated element and inherits the complements of that element.

Ackerman and Webelhuth here are following the standard pre-HPSG3[1] assumption that lexical representations are complete signs, including phonology, content, argument structure, and, crucially, valence. The only kind of information found in phrasal signs that is not found in lexical signs is phrase structure itself, represented by the DAUGHTERS feature. Given the model of the lexicon described in §3.4.1, that means the dividing line between lexicon and syntax falls between valence and phrase structure:

(8) Lexicon

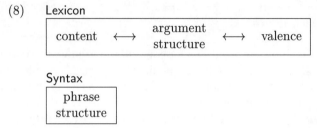

Syntax
```
 phrase
structure
```

Recall that content and argument structure are related by linking constraints, argument structure and valence are related by realization constraints, and valence and phrase structure are related by constructions.

Given this view, not only do argument attraction analyses violate lexical integrity, even the most basic combination of a head with its subcategorized-for dependents will. Lexical adicity prohibits a syntactic rule from making non-monotonic changes to lexical information. If valence is considered part of a lexical entry, any valence cancellation entails a non-monotonic change to lexical information. So, it would appear to be impossible to maintain lexical adicity in a theory like HPSG.

If we look at the kinds of lexical rules that have been proposed in recent work in HPSG, however, the view of grammar pictured in (8) is called into question. The lexical rules ultimately adopted in chapter 3 involve the manipulation of category and/or argument structure. What they specifically do not do is change valence values. These lexical rules are structure preserving in the sense that their outputs conform to the same realization constraints as any other words in the language do. Other lexical rules that have appeared in the literature recently (e.g., Miller and Sag 1997) also have this property, and phenomena that earlier had been accounted for by valence-changing lexical rules have been reanalyzed as realization alternations (see §3.4.1). At this point it seems appropriate to make the following conjecture: lexical representations (lexemes) include argument structure but not valence, and

---

[1]That is, up to chapter 9 of Pollard and Sag 1994.

syntactic representations (words and phrases) include valence but not argument structure. If this is true, then the realization constraints are the only part of the grammar that refer to both argument structure and valence, and they form the interface between the lexicon and the syntax:

(9) Lexicon

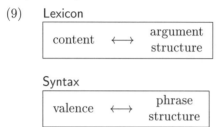

Lexical entries include specifications for content and argument structure, but not for valence. The argument realization principles which map argument structure to valence form the interface between the lexicon and the syntax. A consequence of this is that lexical rules can destructively modify argument structure and constructions can destructively modify valence. That is to say, the argument structure of the output of a lexical rule may differ non-monotonically from that of the input, and the valence of the mother of a phrase may differ non-monotonically from that of the head daughter. This means argument attraction analyses which syntactically combine the valence lists of more than one lexical head pose no problem for lexical adicity.

This division of labor has already been adopted at least in spirit by Bouma et al. (in press), among others. At least two problems remain, however. One technical problem is that the constraints on pronominal binding are generally considered part of 'the syntax,' and, as Pollard and Sag (1994) and Manning (1996) argue, they make crucial reference to argument structure configurations. If argument structures do not play a role in syntactic representations, then it is hard to see what kind of linguistic object the binding constraints could be constraints on. One option, suggested by Ivan Sag (p.c.), would be to roll the binding constraints into the realization constraints. In addition to identifying argument positions in a lexeme with valence positions in a word, the realization constraints could impose binding constraints on words along the lines proposed by Dalrymple (1993) and Koenig (1999a). This would be consistent with their role as the interface between lexical and syntactic representations.

A more serious problem for this view is that not all argument attraction analyses operate on valence structures. Abeillé et al. (1998b) argue on the basis of cliticization facts that some French auxiliaries involve syntactic composition of argument structures. It is interesting to note however that this argument against lexical adicity is based on agreement morphology. Inflection, and in particular agreement, is the most syntactically active of lexical properties, and it is given special syntactic status by, for example, Anderson (1992) and Kathol (1999). It would be interesting to investigate whether this argument composition is crucial, or if the analysis could be restated in terms of valence composition and agreement features. On the other hand, Malouf (1999) presents an analysis of West Greenlandic noun incorporation which is similar to the Gerund Formation Lexical Rule but which requires lexical access to valence information. However, in this case as well alternative analyses may be available (see Sadock 1991, Van Geenhoven 1998, Malouf 1998).

So, while the revised view of the syntax-lexicon interface shown in (9) is not without its shortcomings, none of these problems seems insurmountable. The revised form of the lexical integrity hypothesis outlined in this section therefore is an interesting, more restrictive alternative to the one usually assumed in HPSG work. Whether it accurately characterizes natural language is a question for further research.

4.2.3　Language change

As we saw in §2.4, English verbal gerunds passed through several stages in their development from Old English verbal nouns. This is a common property of diachronic linguistic development: language changes proceed gradually as a change spreads through the grammar. In the course of a change, one often finds hybrid forms that show mixed properties, with some of the characteristics of the original form and some of the arising form.

One instance of a hybrid construction, discussed by Tabor (1994), is found in the development of the degree modifier *sort of*/*kind of*. In Modern English, *sort of* and *kind of* have two common uses. In one, *sort* or *kind* is a noun which combines with a PP headed by *of*:

(10)　a.　They found some sort/kind of cactus on the rim.
　　　　b.　What sort/kind of knife do you need.

This use is first found in Middle English and is quite common by the sixteenth century (Tabor 1994, 140):

(11)　a.　Let vs now see whether sort of these twayn might take most harme.　　　　　　　　　　　　[1529, *whether* = 'which']
　　　　b.　I knowe that sorte of men ryght well.　　　　　　　　[1560]

In the other use, *sort*/*kind of* functions as a degree modifier, much like *somewhat* or *rather*:

(12) a. We are sort/kind of hungry.
      b. He sort/kind of hemmed and hawed.

This use does not appear unambiguously until the nineteenth century:

(13) a. I was kind of provoked at the way you came up.   [1830]
      b. It sort o' stirs one up to hear about old times.   [1833]

This kind of change can be easily modeled in any standard grammatical theory. This shift simply reflects the reanalysis of *sort of* and *kind of* as degree modifiers.

What is challenging about this development is that alongside early examples of the second type, one finds examples that appear to share properties of both uses (Tabor 1994, 180):

(14) a. Its a fine ewnin but its a sort a caad.
          'It's a fine evening, but it's sort of cold.'   [1790]
      b. It seems a sort of foolish to me, tho'   [1855]
      c. Ah'm a sort o' done up wi' walking so much   [1898]

In this use, which died out in most dialects by the early twentieth century, *sort of* and *kind of* function semantically like a degree modifier, but still combine with the determiner *a* like a noun would.

Tabor uses hybrids like this to argue for a continuous model of syntactic categories. If syntactic categories are continuously variable and grammatical change is incremental, one would expect to find many intermediate steps in the course of a categorical change. This hybrid use is more difficult to model given a standard generative theory of grammar. As Tabor (1994, 171) points out:

> Languages containing hybrids are not problematic descriptively, for standard models of grammar in the way that, for example, languages consisting only of strings of the form $a^n b^n c^n$ are problematic for context-free grammars [...] But they are an embarrassment for current categorical theories [...] because they seem to require stipulating ad-hoc new types for forms whose relationships to existing types is systemic. Although Competing Grammars models generate probabilistic hybrid behavior, they exclude hybrid structures.

So, simply adding an arbitrarily large number of additional categories to a discrete category model is not sufficient to explain the behavior of hybrids. However, the general model outlined in chapter 3 at least has the potential to avoid this problem without completely abandoning discrete categories. Hybrids represent types with an unusual combination of syntactic properties inherited from otherwise disjoint supertypes.

Thus, both the regular and irregular nature of hybrids can be modeled in this kind of system.

Suppose we give the Middle English lexicon the partial representation in Figure 21. This is the same as the Modern English lexical hierarchy from Figure 20 on page 133, except that I have added a category for degree modifiers (dm) and, to simplify things, I have omitted the linking dimension. Lexically specified inheritance is shown with a solid line, and inheritance derived by on-line type construction is shown with a dashed line.

In the first stage of the change, *sort* and *kind* are reclassified as degree modifiers. As a minimal change to the grammar, this reclassification introduces the types $sort_2$ and $kind_2$ as in Figure 22. Nothing else changes; specifically, the maximal types $sort_{2w}$ and $kind_{2w}$ that inherit from $sort_2$ and $kind_2$ are subtypes of the same types that $sort_1$ and $kind_1$ are subtypes of. This means that $sort_{2w}$ and $kind_{2w}$ will have some of the properties of degree modifiers and some of the properties of common nouns. This is a very highly marked situation, as a degree modifier would not normally inherit from any of the same supertypes as a common noun. In the third stage of the change, shown in Figure 23, the types $sort_{w3}$ and $kind_{w3}$ are generated by on-line type construction as expected, and so they inherit from the same supertypes as any other degree modifier. Finally, the exceptional types $sort_{2w}$ and $kind_{2w}$ are lost, leaving the common noun and degree modifier uses of *sort of* and *kind of*.

This is, of course, only a first step towards giving an account of language change in HPSG. For instance, nothing here explains why the change might get started in the first place. Tabor (1994, 1998) argues that the qualitative aspects of a change are driven by its quantitative aspects. That is, shifts in frequency facilitate or even cause shifts in categorization. It would be interesting to see whether a grammatical model like the one presented here, augmented with frequency information (Abney 1997, Riezler 1996, Riezler 1999), could account for the quantitative facts Tabor discusses.

One clear difference between the two models is that for Tabor categories are strictly extensional. Words are located in the category space strictly on the basis of their distribution. Words with similar distributions belong to closely related categories, while words with different distributions belong to more distantly related categories. In the present analysis, words may be classified strictly on the basis of their distribution, but they need not be. A word may belong to a category without sharing any properties of that category if its lexical entry overrides all the information inherited from its supertype. This would be highly marked

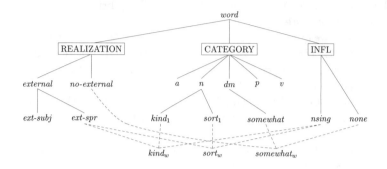

FIGURE 21 English lexicon c. 1500

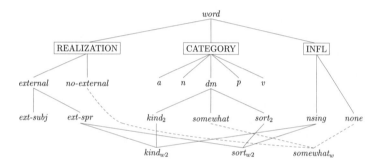

FIGURE 22 English lexicon c. 1800

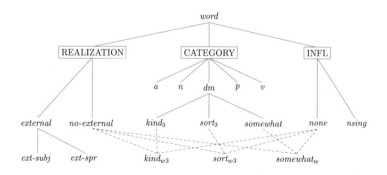

FIGURE 23 English lexicon c. 1900

(see §1.5), and we would not expect to find any words that actually behave this way. Indeed, it is hard to say how the analyst or the language learner could know that a word belongs to a certain category if there is no evidence for it. However, this is a representational possibility left open by the theory, and it would be interesting to see whether it provides evidence for or against either model.

In general, there is a close relationship between the fine-grained category theory presented here and the continuous category spaces of connectionist and statistical models like Tabor's or Schütze's (1997). Just intuitively, a model with an indefinite number of discrete categories must come out to pretty much the same thing as a model with a finite number of actual linguistic elements placed in a continuous category space. If that is true, then it is an important result, since it might be a way of bringing together the best features of symbolic and connectionist methods.

4.3 Conclusions

We started out this investigation with a question about English verbal gerunds: are they nouns are or they verbs? The conclusion we reached was that this is an ill-formed question. Gerunds as a class share certain properties with other classes of words, and while it is interesting to see what properties gerunds share with which classes of words and why, whether gerunds are nouns or verbs, or both or neither, is a question of terminology, not grammatical theory.

A natural consequence of this approach is the conclusion that parts of speech as such play no role in the grammar. Instead, grammatical processes are sensitive to a number of independently varying types of information. Relationships among classes of words are expressed in the lexicon by means of a system of cross-cutting hierarchical types placing constraints on one or more of these dimensions of linguistic information.

But, it is not enough to simply deconstruct the notion of syntactic category. It may be true that in principle dimensions like lexical category, semantic type, and valence can vary independently, and it seems that mixed categorial behavior is more common than is typically appreciated. However, it remains a fact that in practice these dimensions almost always covary. Normal nouns do not take accusative subjects or objects, and normal verbs do not take genitive specifiers. Even if parts of speech are external to the synchronic grammar, they do exist as higher order generalizations across types in the lexicon. That is, a syntactic category like "noun", in the traditional sense, does not correspond to any one lexical type, but instead is more like a region within the hierarchical lexicon. The boundaries of this region may be fuzzy (perhaps in the formal sense of Zadeh 1965), some types may be better members of the class than others, and the regions may overlap and run together. This does not mean abandoning formal grammar: each individual type is still discrete and determinate. It is only these meta-generalizations over types that are vague. Further, while these regions are not relevant to a description of a synchronic competence grammar, that they are very important to understanding language acquisition and language change. Even though parts of speech are not first class objects in the theory of grammar, they do exist and their cohesiveness is maintained through a combination of functional and historical pressures. In this way, this view of syntactic categories has the potential to clarify the relationship between formal, categorical theories of grammar and less discrete models of language use and language change.

References

Abeillé, Anne, Danièle Godard, Philip Miller, and Ivan A. Sag. 1998a. French bounded dependencies. In *Romance in HPSG*, ed. Luca Dini and Sergio Balari. 1–54. Stanford: CSLI Publications.

Abeillé, Anne, Danièle Godard, and Ivan A. Sag. 1998b. Two kinds of composition in French complex predicates. In *Complex Predicates in Nonderivational Syntax.* Syntax and Semantics, Vol. 30, 1–42. New York: Academic Press.

Abney, Steven P. 1987. *The English Noun Phrase in its Sentential Aspect.* Doctoral dissertation, MIT.

Abney, Steven P. 1997. Stochastic attribute-value grammars. *Computational Linguistics* 23:597–618.

Ackerman, Farrell, and Gert Webelhuth. 1998. *A Theory of Predicates.* Stanford: CSLI Publications.

Akmajian, Adrian. 1977. The complement structure of perception verbs in an autonoumous syntax framework. In *Formal Syntax*, ed. Peter Culicover, Thomas Wasow, and Adrian Akmajian. 427–460. New York: Academic Press.

Allegranza, Valerio. 1998. Determiners as functors: NP structure in Italian. In *Romance in HPSG*, ed. Luca Dini and Sergio Balari. 55–108. Stanford: CSLI Publications.

Anderson, John M. 1997. *A notional theory of syntactic categories.* Cambridge: Cambridge University Press.

Anderson, Stephen R. 1992. *A-Morphous Morphology.* Cambridge: Cambridge University Press.

Aoun, Youssef. 1981. Parts of speech: a case of redistribution. In *Theory of Markedness in Generative Grammar*, ed. A. Belletti, L. Brandi, and L. Rizzi. 3–24. Pisa: Scoula Normale Superiore di Pisa.

Aronoff, Mark. 1976. *Word Formation in Generative Grammar.* Cambridge, MA: MIT Press.

Baker, Mark C. 1985. Syntactic affixation and English gerunds. In *Proceedings of the West Coast Conference on Formal Linguistics*, 1–11.

Baker, Mark C. 1988. *Incorporation*. Chicago: University of Chicago Press.

Baker, Mark C., Kyle Johnson, and Ian Roberts. 1989. Passive arguments raised. *Linguistic Inquiry* 20:219–251.

Barwise, Jon, and John Perry. 1983. *Situations and Attitudes*. Cambridge, MA: MIT Press.

Bates, Elizabeth, and Brian MacWhinney. 1989. Functionalism and the Competition Model. In *The Crosslinguistic Study of Sentence Processing*, ed. Brian MacWhinney and Elizabeth Bates. 3–73. Cambridge University Press.

Bernstein, Judy. 1993. *Topics in the Syntax of Nominal Structure Across Romance*. Doctoral dissertation, CUNY.

Beyer, Stephan V. 1992. *The Classical Tibetan Language*. Albany: SUNY Press.

Bird, Steven. 1995. *Computational Phonology: A Constraint-Based Approach*. Cambridge University Press.

Blevins, James P., and Ivan A. Sag. 1996. Constituent sharing and nonconstituent coordination. University of Alberta and Stanford University.

Bloomfield, Leonard. 1933. *Language*. University of Chicago Press.

Bodomo, Adams B. 1997. *The Structure of Dagaare*. Stanford: CSLI Publications.

Borsley, Robert D. 1995. On some similarities and differences between Welsh and Syrian Arabic. *Linguistics* 33:99–122.

Borsley, Robert D., and Jaklin Kornfilt. 2000. Mixed extended projections. In *The Nature and Function of Syntactic Categories*, ed. Robert D. Borsley. Syntax and Semantics, Vol. 32, 101–132. New York: Academic Press.

Bouma, Gosse. 1993. *Nonmonotonicity and Categorial Unification Grammar*. Doctoral dissertation, Rijksuniversiteit Groningen.

Bouma, Gosse, Robert Malouf, and Ivan A. Sag. in press. Satisfying constraints on extraction and adjunction. *Natural Language and Linguistic Theory*.

Bresnan, Joan. 1995. Lexicality and Argument Structure. Paper presented at the Paris Syntax and Semantics Conference. URL http://www-lfg.stanford.edu/~bresnan/paris.ps.

Bresnan, Joan. 1997. Mixed categories as head sharing constructions. In *Proceedings of the LFG97 Conference*, ed. Miriam Butt and Tracy Holloway King. Stanford. CSLI Publications. URL http://csli-publications.stanford.edu/LFG2/lfg97.html.

Bresnan, Joan. 1998. Morphology competes with syntax: explaining typological variation in weak crossover effects. In *Is the Best Good Enough? Proceedings from the Workshop on Optimality in Syntax*, ed. Pilar Barbosa, Danny Fox, Paul Hagstrom, Martha McGinnis, and David Pesetsky, 59–92. MIT Press and MIT Working Papers in Linguistics.

Bresnan, Joan, and Sam A. Mchombo. 1995. The lexical integrity principle: evidence from Bantu. *Natural Language and Linguistic Theory* 13:181–254.

Briscoe, Ted, Ann Copestake, and Alex Lascarides. 1995. Blocking. In *Computational Lexical Semantics*, ed. P. St. Dizier and E. Viegas. 273–301. Cambridge University Press.

Carpenter, Bob. 1991. The generative power of categorial grammars and head-driven phrase structure grammars with lexical rules. *Computational Linguistics* 17:301–314.

Carpenter, Bob. 1992. *The Logic of Typed Feature Structures*. Cambridge University Press.

Chomsky, Noam. 1957. *Syntactic Structures*. The Hague: Mouton.

Chomsky, Noam. 1965. *Aspects of the Theory of Syntax*. Cambridge: MIT Press.

Chomsky, Noam. 1970. Remarks on nominalizations. In *Readings in English Transformational Grammar*, ed. R. Jacobs and P. Rosenbaum. 184–221. Waltham, Ma: Ginn.

Chomsky, Noam. 1975. *The Logical Structure of Linguistic Theory*. New York: Plenum Press. Distributed as a mimeograph in 1955.

Chomsky, Noam. 1981. *Lectures on Government and Binding*. Dordrecht: Foris.

Chomsky, Noam. 1986. *Barriers*. Cambridge: MIT Press.

Chomsky, Noam. 1993. A minimalist program for linguistic theory. In *The View frrom Building 20*, ed. Kenneth Hale and Samuel Jay Keyser. 1–52. Cambridge: MIT Press.

Chomsky, Noam, and Howard Lasnik. 1977. Filters and control. *Linguistic Inquiry* 8:425–504.

Cinque, Guglielmo. 1994. On the evidence for partial N-movement in the Romance DP. In *Paths Towards Universal Grammar*, ed. Guglielmo Cinque, Jan Koster, Jean-Yves Pollock, Luigi Rizzi, and Raffaelle Zanuttini. 85–110. Washington: Georgetown University Press.

Comrie, Bernard. 1976. The syntax of action nominals: a cross-language study. *Lingua* 40:177–201.

Comrie, Bernard. 1989. *Language Universals and Linguistic Typology.* Chicago: University of Chicago Press. second edition.

Cooper, Robin. 1983. *Quantification and Syntactic Theory.* Dordrecht: Reidel.

Crisma, Paola. 1993. On adjective placement in Romance and Germanic event nominals. *Rivista di Grammatica Generativa* 18:61–100.

Crisma, Paola. 1995. On the configurational nature of adjectival modification. In *Grammatical Theory and Romance Languages*, ed. Karen Zagona. 59–71. Amsterdam: John Benjamins.

Croft, William. 1990a. A conceptual framework for grammatical categories. *Journal of Semantics* 7:245–279.

Croft, William. 1990b. *Typology and Universals.* Cambridge: Cambridge University Press.

Croft, William. 1991. *Syntactic Categories and Grammatical Relations.* University of Chicago Press.

Croft, William. 1995. Autonomy and functionalist linguistics. *Language* 71:490–532.

Dal, Ingerid. 1952. Zur Entstehung des englischen Participium Praesentis auf *-ing*. *Norsk Tidsskrift for Sprogvidenskap* 16:5–116.

Dalrymple, Mary. 1993. *The Syntax of Anaphoric Binding.* Stanford: CSLI Publications.

Davis, Anthony R. 1996. *Lexical Semantics and Linking in the Hierarchical Lexicon.* Doctoral dissertation, Stanford University. URL http://www-linguistics.stanford.edu/~tdavis/thesis-ps.html.

Davis, Anthony R., and Jean-Pierre Koenig. 2000. Linking as constraints on word classes in a hierarchical lexicon. *Language* 76:56–91.

Di Sciullo, Anna-Maria, and Edwin Williams. 1987. *On the Definition of Word.* Cambridge: MIT Press.

Diesing, Molly. 1992. *Indefinites.* Cambridge: MIT Press.

Dixon, R. M. W. 1988. *A Grammar of Boumaa Fijian.* Chicago: University of Chicago Press.

Donner, Morton. 1986. The gerund in Middle English. *English Studies* 67:394–400.

Dowty, David R. 1989. On the semantic content of the notion 'thematic role'. In *Properties, Types and Meaning II*, ed. Gennaro Chierchia, Barbara Partee, and Raymond Turner. 69–129. Dordrecht: Kluwer.

DuBois, John W. 1985. Competing motivations. In *Iconicity in Syntax*, ed. John Haiman. 343–365. Amsterdam: John Benjamins.

Emonds, Joseph. 1976. *A Transformational Approach to English Syntax.* New York: Academic Press.

Emonds, Joseph. 1987. Parts of speech in generative grammar. *Linguistic Analysis* 17:3–42.

Erteschik-Shir, Nomi. 1973. *On the Nature of Island Constraints.* Doctoral dissertation, MIT.

Fassi Fehri, Abdelkader. 1993. *Issues in the Structure of Arabic Clauses and Words.* Dordrecht: Kluwer.

Fiengo, Robert, and James Higginbotham. 1981. Opacity in NP. *Linguistic Analysis* 7:395–421.

Fillmore, Charles J. 1985. Syntactic intrusions and the notion of grammatical construction. In *Proceedings of the Berkeley Linguistics Society*, 73–86.

Fillmore, Charles J. 1999. Inversion and constructional inheritance. In *Lexical and Constructional Aspects of Linguistic Explanation*, ed. Gert Webelhuth, Andreas Kathol, and Jean-Pierre Koenig. 113–128. Stanford: CSLI Publications.

Fillmore, Charles J., and Paul Kay. to appear. *Construction Grammar.* Stanford: CSLI Publications. URL http://www.icsi.berkeley.edu/~kay/bcg/ConGram.html.

Fillmore, Charles J., Paul Kay, and Mary Catherine O'Connor. 1988. Regularity and idiomaticity in grammatical constructions: the case of *let alone*. *Language* 64:501–538.

Flickinger, Daniel. 1987. *Lexical Rules in the Hierarchical Lexicon.* Doctoral dissertation, Stanford University.

Foley, William A., and Robert D. Van Valin. 1984. *Functional Syntax and Universal Grammar.* Cambridge: Cambridge University Press.

Frances, W. Nelson. 1964. A standard sample of present-day English for use with digital computers. Report to the U.S Office of Education on Cooperative Research Project No. E–007.

Gazdar, Gerald, Ewan Klein, Geoffrey K. Pullum, and Ivan A. Sag. 1985. *Generalized Phrase Structure Grammar.* Cambridge: Harvard University Press.

Gazdar, Gerald, Geoffrey Pullum, and Ivan A. Sag. 1982. Auxiliaries and related phenomena in a restrictive theory of grammar. *Language* 58:591–638.

Gerdts, Donna B. 1992. Mapping Halkomelem grammatical relations. *Linguistics* 31:591–622.

Ginzburg, Jonathan. 1992. *Questions, Queries, and Facts: A Semantics and Pragmatics for Interrogatives.* Doctoral dissertation, Stanford University.

Ginzburg, Jonathan, and Ivan A. Sag. 1998. English interrogative constructions. Hebrew University and Stanford University.

Goldberg, Adele. 1995. *Constructions: a Construction Grammar Approach to Argument Structure*. University of Chicago Press.

Green, Georgia. 1997. Modelling grammar growth: Universal grammar without innate principles or parameters. Paper presented at GALA97 Conference on Language Acquisition, Edinburgh. URL `http://lees.cogsci.uiuc.edu/~green/edinout.ps`.

Greenberg, Joseph H. 1966a. *Language Universals*. Janua Linguarum Series Minor, No. 59. The Hague: Mouton.

Greenberg, Joseph H. 1966b. Some universals of grammar with particular reference to the order of meaningful elements. In *Universals of Grammar*, ed. Joseph H. Greenberg. 73–113. Cambridge: MIT Press.

Greenberg, Joseph H. 1990. Two approaches to language universals. In *On Language: Selected Writings of Joseph H. Greenberg*, ed. Keith Denning and Suzanne Kemmer. 702–720. Stanford: Stanford University Press.

Grimshaw, Jane. 1981. Form, function, and the language acquisition device. In *The Logical Problem of Language Acquisition*, ed. C.L. Baker and J. McCarthy. 165–182. Cambridge: MIT Press.

Hale, Ken, and Paul Platero. 1986. Parts of speech. In *Features and Projections*, ed. Pieter Muysken and Henk van Riemsdijk. 31–40. Dordrecht: Foris.

Halpern, Aaron. 1995. *On the placement and morphology of clitics*. Stanford: CSLI Publications.

Hankamer, Jorge. 1979. *Deletion in coordinate structure*. New York: Garland. Originally appeared as a 1971 Yale PhD dissertation.

Hankamer, Jorge, and Ivan A. Sag. 1976. Deep and surface anaphora. *Linguistic Inquiry* 7:391–426.

Hinrichs, Erhard, and Tsuneko Nakazawa. 1989. Flipped out: Aux in German. In *Proceedings of the Chicago Linguistics Society*, 193–202.

Hinrichs, Erhard, and Tsuneko Nakazawa. 1990. Subcategorization and VP structure in German. In *Proceedings of the Third Symposium on Germanic Linguistics*, ed. Shaun Hughes and Joe Salmons. Amsterdam. Benjamins.

Horn, George M. 1975. On the nonsentential nature of the POSS-ing construction. *Linguistic Analysis* 1:333–388.

Houston, Ann. 1989. The English gerund: syntactic change and discourse function. In *Language Change and Variation*, ed. Ralph W.

Fasold and Deborah Schiffrin. 173–195. Amsterdam: John Benjamins.

Jackendoff, Ray. 1972. *Semantic interpretation in generative grammar.* Cambridge: MIT Press.

Jackendoff, Ray. 1974. A deep structure projection rule. *Linguistic Inquiry* 5:481–506.

Jackendoff, Ray. 1977. *X̄ Syntax: A Study of Phrase Structure.* Cambridge: MIT Press.

Jackendoff, Ray. 1997. *The Architecture of the Language Faculty.* Cambridge, MA: MIT Press.

Jørgensen, Eric. 1981. Gerund and *to*-infinitives after 'it is (of) no use', 'it is no good', and 'it is useless'. *English Studies* 62:156–163.

Kaiser, Lizanne. 1997. CPR for Korean Type III nominalizations. In *Yale A-morphous Linguistics Essays*, ed. Lizanne Kaiser. 89–97. Department of Linguistics, Yale University.

Kaiser, Lizanne. 1999. *The Morphosyntax of Clausal Nominalization Constructions.* Doctoral dissertation, Yale University.

Kaplan, Ronald M., and Joan Bresnan. 1982. Lexical-Functional Grammar: a formal system for grammatical representation. In *The Mental Representation of Grammatical Relations*, ed. Joan Bresnan. MIT Press.

Kathol, Andreas. 1999. Agreement and the syntax-morphology interface in HPSG. In *Studies in Current Phrase Structure Grammar*, ed. Robert D. Levine and Georgia Green. 223–274. Cambridge University Press.

Kay, Paul. 1994. Anaphoric binding in Construction Grammar. In *Proceedings of the Berkeley Linguistics Society*, ed. Susanne Gahl, Andy Dolbey, and Christopher Johnson, 283–299.

Kay, Paul, and Charles J. Fillmore. 1999. Grammatical constructions and linguistic generalizations: The *What's X doing Y?* construction. *Language* 75:1–33.

Kim, Jong-Bok. 1995a. English negation from a non-derivational perspective. In *Proceedings of the Berkeley Linguistics Society*, ed. Jocelyn Ahlers, Leela Bilmes, Joshua S. Guenter, Barbara A. Kaiser, and Ju Namkung, 186–196.

Kim, Jong-Bok. 1995b. *The grammar of negation: a lexicalist, constraint-based perspective.* Doctoral dissertation, Stanford University.

Kim, Jong-Bok. 1995c. On the existence of NegP in Korean. In *Proceedings of the 6th Harvard International Symposium on Korean Linguistics.*

Kim, Jong-Bok, and Ivan A. Sag. 1995. The parametric variation of English and French negation. In *Proceedings of the West Coast Conference on Formal Linguistics*, 303–317.

King, Paul John. 1997. A formalism for HPSG'94. Universität Tübingen, URL http://www.sfs.nphil.uni-tuebingen.de/~king/docs/hpsg94.ps.gz.

Kiparsky, Paul. 1982. Lexical morphology and phonology. In *Linguistics in the Morning Calm*, ed. The Linguistic Society of Korea. 3–91. Hanshin Publishing Co.

Kirby, Simon. 1997. Competing motivations and emergence: explaining implicational hierarchies. *Language Typology* 1:5–32.

Koenig, Jean-Pierre. 1994. *Lexical Underspecification and the Syntax/Semantics Interface*. Doctoral dissertation, UC Berkeley.

Koenig, Jean-Pierre. 1999a. Inside-out constraints and description languages for HPSG. In *Lexical and Constructional Aspects of Linguistic Explanation*, ed. Gert Webelhuth, Andreas Kathol, and Jean-Pierre Koenig. 265–280. Stanford: CSLI Publications.

Koenig, Jean-Pierre. 1999b. *Lexical Relations*. Stanford: CSLI Publications.

Koenig, Jean-Pierre, and Dan Jurafsky. 1994. Type underspecification and on-line type construction. In *Proceedings of the West Coast Conference on Formal Linguistics*.

Koptevskaja-Tamm, Maria. 1993. *Nominalizations*. London: Routledge.

Kornai, András, and Geoffrey K. Pullum. 1990. The X-bar theory of phrase structure. *Language* 66:24–50.

Kuno, Susumo. 1973. Constraints on internal clauses and sentential objects. *Linguistic Inquiry* 4:363–385.

Lakoff, George. 1987. *Women, Fire, and Dangerous Things*. Chicago: University of Chicago Press.

Lambrecht, Knud. 1990. 'What me worry?' Mad magazine sentences revisited. In *Proceedings of the Berkeley Linguistics Society*, 215–228.

Langacker, Ronald W. 1973. *Language and its Structure*. New York: Harcourt Brace Jovanovich. 2nd edition.

Langacker, Ronald W. 1987a. *Foundations of Cognitive Grammar*. Stanford: Stanford University Press.

Langacker, Ronald W. 1987b. Nouns and verbs. *Language* 63:53–94.

Lapointe, Steven G. 1993. Dual lexical categories and the syntax of mixed category phrases. In *Proceedings of the Eastern States Conference of Linguistics*, ed. A. Kathol and M. Bernstein, 199–210.

Larson, Richard K. 1988. On the double object construction. *Linguistic Inquiry* 19:335–391.

Lascarides, Alex, Ted Briscoe, Nicholas Asher, and Ann Copestake. 1996. Order independent and persistent typed default unification. *Linguistics and Philosophy* 19:1–89.

Lascarides, Alex, and Ann Copestake. 1999. Default representation in constraint-based frameworks. *Computational Linguistics* 25:55–105.

Lees, Robert B. 1960. *The Grammar of English nominalizations*. Doctoral dissertation, Massachusetts Institute of Technology.

Lefebvre, Claire, and Pieter Muysken. 1988. *Mixed Categories*. Dordrecht: Kluwer.

Lichtenberk, Frantisek. 1991. On the gradualness of grammaticalization. In *Approaches to Grammaticalization*, ed. Elizabeth C. Traugott and Bernd Heine. 37–80. Amsterdam: John Benjamins.

Longobardi, Giuseppe. 1994. Reference and proper names: A theory of N-movement in syntax and logical form. *Linguistic Inquiry* 25:609–665.

Macnamara, John. 1982. *Names for things: a study of human learning*. Cambridge: MIT Press.

Malouf, Robert. 1998. *Mixed Categories in the Hierarchical Lexicon*. Doctoral dissertation, Stanford University.

Malouf, Robert. 1999. West Greenlandic noun incorporation in a monohierarchical theory of grammar. In *Lexical and Constructional Aspects of Linguistic Explanation*, ed. Gert Webelhuth, Andreas Kathol, and Jean-Pierre Koenig. 47–62. Stanford: CSLI Publications.

Malouf, Robert. 2000. Verbal gerunds as mixed categories in Head-Driven Phrase Structure Grammar. In *The Nature and Function of Syntactic Categories*, ed. Robert D. Borsley. Syntax and Semantics, Vol. 32, 133–166. New York: Academic Press.

Manning, Christopher D. 1996. *Ergativity: Argument Structure and Grammatical Relations*. Stanford: CSLI Publications.

Manning, Christopher D., and Ivan A. Sag. 1999. Dissociations between argument structure and grammatical relations. In *Lexical and Constructional Aspects of Linguistic Explanation*, ed. Gert Webelhuth, Andreas Kathol, and Jean-Pierre Koenig. 63–78. Stanford: CSLI Publications.

Marantz, Alec. 1978. Embedded sentences are not noun phrases. In *Proceedings of the North Eastern Linguistics Society*, ed. Mark J. Stein, 112–122. Amherst, Ma. Graduate Linguistic Student Association, University of Massachusetts.

McCawley, James D. 1982. The nonexistence of syntactic categories. In *Thirty Million Theories of Grammar.* University of Chicago Press.

McCawley, James D. 1988. *The Syntactic Phenomena of English.* University of Chicago Press.

Menuzzi, Sergio. 1994. Adjectival positions inside DP. In *Linguistics in the Netherlands 1994,* ed. Reineke Bok-Bennema and Crit Cremers. 127–138. Amsterdam: John Benjamins.

Meurers, W. Detmar. 1994. On implementing an HPSG theory. In *Partial-VP and Split-NP Topicalization in German,* ed. Erhard W. Hinrichs, W. Detmar Meurers, and Tsuneko Nakazawa. Arbeitspapiere des SFB 340, No. 58. Universität Tübingen. URL http://www.sfs.nphil.uni-tuebingen.de/~dm/on-implementing.html.

Michael, Ian. 1970. *English Grammatical Categories and the Tradition to 1800.* Cambridge: Cambridge University Press.

Miller, Philip, and Ivan A. Sag. 1997. French clitic movement without clitics or movement. *Natural Language and Linguistic Theory* 15:573–639.

Milsark, Gary L. 1988. Singl-*ing. Linguistic Inquiry* 19:611–634.

Neumann, Günter. 1994. Application of explanation-based learning for efficient processing of constraint based grammars. In *Proceedings of the Tenth IEEE Conference on Artificial Intelligence for Applications,* 208–215. San Antonio, Texas, March.

Newmeyer, Frederick J. 1998. *Language Form and Language Function.* Cambridge: MIT Press.

Newmeyer, Frederick J. 2000. The discrete nature of syntactic categories: against a prototype-based account. In *The Nature and Function of Syntactic Categories,* ed. Robert D. Borsley. Syntax and Semantics, Vol. 32, 221–250. New York: Academic Press.

Orgun, C. Orhan. 1996. *Sign-Based Morphology and Phonology with special attention to Optimality Theory.* Doctoral dissertation, UC Berkeley.

Osherson, Daniel, and Edward Smith. 1981. On the adequacy of prototype theory as a theory of concepts. *Cognition* 9:35–58.

Pesetsky, David. 1981. *Paths and categories.* Doctoral dissertation, MIT.

Pinker, Steven. 1982. A theory of the acquisition of lexical interpretive grammars. In *The Mental Representation of Grammatical Relations,* ed. Joan Bresnan. 655–726. Cambridge: MIT Press.

Pinker, Steven. 1989. *Learnability and cognition.* Cambridge: MIT Press.

Pinker, Steven. 1998. Words and rules. *Lingua* 106:219–242.

Pollard, Carl. 1996. The nature of constraint-based grammar. Paper presented at the Pacific Asia Conference on Language, Information, and Computation, Seoul.

Pollard, Carl, and Ivan A. Sag. 1987. *Information-based Syntax and Semantics.* Stanford: CSLI Publications.

Pollard, Carl, and Ivan A. Sag. 1994. *Head-Driven Phrase Structure Grammar.* Chicago and Stanford: University of Chicago Press and CSLI Publications.

Pollard, Carl, and Eun Jung Yoo. 1998. Quantifiers, *wh*-phrases, and a theory of argument selection. *Journal of Linguistics* 34:415–446.

Pollock, Jean-Yves. 1989. Verb movement, Universal Grammar, and the structure of IP. *Linguistic Inquiry* 20:365–424.

Portner, Paul H. 1992. *Situation Theory and the Semantics of Propositional Expressions.* Doctoral dissertation, University of Massachusetts, Amherst. Distributed by the University of Massachusetts Graduate Linguistic Student Association.

Pullum, Geoffrey K. 1989. Formal linguistics meets the boojum. *Natural Language and Linguistic Theory* 7:137–143.

Pullum, Geoffrey K. 1991. English nominal gerund phrases as noun phrases with verb-phrase heads. *Linguistics* 29:763–799.

Pullum, Geoffrey K., and Arnold M. Zwicky. 1991. Condition duplication, paradigm homonymy, and transconstructional constraints. In *Proceedings of the Berkeley Linguistics Society,* 252–266.

Quirk, Randolf, Sidney Greenbaum, Geoffrey Leech, and Jan Svartvik. 1985. *A Comprehensive Grammar of the English Language.* London: Longman.

Reape, Michael. 1994. Domain Union and Word Order Variation in German. In *German in Head-driven Phrase Structure Grammar,* ed. John Nerbonne, Klaus Netter, and Carl Pollard. 151–197. Stanford: CSLI Publications.

Reuland, Eric. 1983. Governing -*ing. Linguistic Inquiry* 14:101–136.

Richter, Frank. 2000. *A Mathematical Formalism for Linguistic Theories with an Application in Head-Driven Phrase Structure Grammar.* Doctoral dissertation, Universität Tübingen.

Riehemann, Susanne Z. 1998. Type-based derivational morphology. *Journal of Comparative Germanic Linguistics* 2:49–77.

Riezler, Stefan. 1996. Quantitative constraint logic programming for weighted grammar applications. In *Logical Aspects of Computational Linguistics (LACL '96),* ed. Christian Retoré. 346–365. Berlin: Springer.

Riezler, Stefan. 1999. *Probabilistic Constraint Logic Programming*. Doctoral dissertation, Universität Tübingen.

Rosch, Eleanor. 1973. Natural categories. *Cognitive Psychology* 4:328–50.

Rosch, Eleanor. 1978. Principles of categorization. In *Cognition and Categorization*, ed. E. Rosch and B. B. Lloyd. 24–48. Hillsdale: Lawrence Erlbaum.

Rosenbaum, Peter. 1967. *The Grammar of English Predicate Complement Constructions*. Doctoral dissertation, Massachusetts Institute of Technology.

Ross, John R. 1967. *Constraints on Variables in Syntax*. Doctoral dissertation, Massachusetts Institute of Technology.

Ross, John R. 1972. Endstation Hauptwort: the category squish. In *Papers from the Eighth Regional Meeting*, ed. Paul M. Peranteau, Judith N. Levi, and Gloria C. Phares, 316–328. Chicago Linguistics Society.

Ross, John R. 1973a. A fake NP squish. In *New Ways of Analyzing Variation in English*, ed. C.-J. N. Bailey and R. Shuy. 96–140. Washington: Georgetown University Press.

Ross, John R. 1973b. Nouniness. In *Three dimensions of linguistic theory*, ed. Osamu Fujimura. 137–258. Tokyo: Tokyo Institute for Advanced Studies of Language.

Rumelhart, David E., and James L. McClelland. 1986. *Parallel Distributed Processing*. Cambridge: MIT Press.

Sadock, Jerrold M. 1991. *Autolexical Syntax*. Chicago: University of Chicago Press.

Sag, Ivan A. 1976. *Deletion and Logical Form*. Doctoral dissertation, MIT.

Sag, Ivan A. 1996. Constraint-based extraction (without a trace). *Ene [Korean Journal of Linguistics]* 21:57–91.

Sag, Ivan A. 1997. English relative clause constructions. *Journal of Linguistics* 33:431–484.

Sag, Ivan A., and Janet D. Fodor. 1994. Extraction without traces. In *Proceedings of the West Coast Conference on Formal Linguistics*, 365–384.

Sag, Ivan A., Gerald Gazdar, Thomas Wasow, and Steven Weisler. 1985. Coordination and how to distinguish categories. *Natural Language and Linguistic Theory* 3:117–172.

Sag, Ivan A., and Carl Pollard. 1991. An integrated theory of complement control. *Language* 67:63–113.

Sag, Ivan A., and Thomas Wasow. 1999. *Syntactic Theory: A Formal Introduction*. Stanford: CSLI Publications.

Sapir, Edward. 1921. *Language*. San Diego: Harcourt Brace.

Saussure, Ferdinand de. 1916. *Cours de Linguistique Générale*. Paris: Payet. Translated by W. Baskin. 1959. New York: McGraw Hill.

Schachter, Paul. 1976. A nontransformational analysis of gerundive nominals in English. *Linguistic Inquiry* 7:205–241.

Schütze, Hinrich. 1997. *Ambiguity Resolution in Language Learning*. Stanford: CSLI Publications.

Searle, John. 1969. *Speech Acts*. Cambridge: Cambridge University Press.

Shieber, Stuart M. 1986. A simple reconstruction of GPSG. In *Proceedings of the Eleventh International Conference on Computational Linguistics (COLING-86)*, 211–215. Bonn, Germany.

Silverstein, Michael. 1993. Of nominatives and datives: universal grammar from the bottom up. In *Advances in Role and Reference Grammar*, ed. Jr. Robert D. Van Valin. 465–498. Amsterdam: John Benjamins.

Smets, Martine. 1999. Unification-based paradigmatic morphology. Paper presented at the Tenth Meeting of Computational Linguistics in the Netherlands (CLIN'99).

Tabor, Whitney. 1994. *Syntactic Innovation: A Connectionist Model*. Doctoral dissertation, Stanford University.

Tabor, Whitney. 1998. Continuity in language change: implications for the theory of grammar. University of Connecticut.

Tajima, Matsuji. 1985. *The Syntactic Developent of the Gerund in Middle English*. Tokyo: Nan'un-do.

Taylor, John R. 1995. *Linguistic Categorization*. Oxford: Oxford University Press. second edition.

Tiersma, Peter Meijes. 1982. Local and general markedness. *Language* 58:832–849.

Valois, Daniel. 1991. *The Internal Syntax of DP*. Doctoral dissertation, UCLA.

Van Geenhoven, Veerle. 1998. *Semantic Incorporation and Indefinite Descriptions: Semantic and Syntactic Aspects of Noun Incorporation in West Greenlandic*. Stanford: CSLI Publications.

van Hoek, Karen. 1997. *Anaphora and Conceptual Structure*. Chicago: University of Chicago Press.

van Riemsdijk, Henk. 1983. A note on German adjectives. In *Linguistic Categories: Auxiliaries and Related Puzzles*, ed. Frank Heny and Barry Richards. 223–252. Dordrecht: Reidel.

Wasow, Thomas, and Thomas Roeper. 1972. On the subject of gerunds. *Foundations of Language* 8:44–61.

Webelhuth, Gert. 1992. *Principles and Parameters of Syntactic Saturation.* New York: Oxford University Press.

Wechsler, Stephen. 1995. *The Semantic Basis of Argument Structure.* Stanford: CSLI Publications.

Wescoat, Michael T. 1994. Phrase structure, lexical sharing, partial ordering, and the English gerund. In *Proceedings of the Berkeley Linguistics Society,* ed. Susanne Gahl, Andy Dolbey, and Christopher Johnson, 587–598.

Wescoat, Michael T. 1996. Hindi and the typology of noun incorporation: an analysis with lexical sharing. Paper presented at the 1996 LSA meeting.

Whorf, Benjamin Lee. 1945. Grammatical categories. *Language* 21:1–11.

Williams, Edwin. 1975. Small clauses in English. In *Syntax and Semantics,* ed. J. Kimball. 249–273. New York: Academic Press.

Wintner, Shuly. in press. Definiteness in the Hebrew noun phrase. *Journal of Linguistics.*

Wittgenstein, Ludwig. 1953. *Philosophical Investigations.* New York: Macmillan. Translated by G.E.M. Anscombe. 1968.

XTAG Research Group. 1995. A Lexicalized Tree Adjoining Grammar for English. IRCS Report 95-03. Philadelphia: University of Pennsylvania.

Yohe, Tom, and George Newall. 1996. *Schoolhouse Rock!: The Official Guide.* Hyperion.

Yoon, James Hye Suk. 1996. Nominal gerund phrases in English as phrasal zero derivations. *Linguistics* 34:329–356.

Zadeh, Lofti Asker. 1965. Fuzzy sets. *Information and Control* 8:338–353.

Zajac, Rémi. 1992. Inheritance and constraint-based grammar formalisms. *Computational Linguistics* 18:159–182.

Zucchi, Alessandro. 1993. *The Language of Propositions and Events.* Dordrecht: Kluwer.

Zwicky, Arnold M. 1985. Heads. *Journal of Linguistics* 21:1–29.

Zwicky, Arnold M. 1987. Suppressing the Z's. *Journal of Linguistics* 23:133–148.

Zwicky, Arnold M. 1994. Dealing out meaning: fundamentals of syntactic constructions. In *Proceedings of the Berkeley Linguistics Society,* ed. Susanne Gahl, Andy Dolbey, and Christopher Johnson, 611–625.

Zwicky, Arnold M., and Nancy S. Levin. 1980. You don't have to. *Linguistic Inquiry* 11:631–636.

Zwicky, Arnold M., and Geoffrey K. Pullum. 1983. Cliticization vs. inflection: English *n't*. *Language* 59:502–513.

Zwicky, Arnold M., and Geoffrey K. Pullum. 1996. Functional restriction: English possessives. Paper presented at 1996 LSA meeting.

Index